LOVE, MARRIAGE, AND RIGHTEOUSNESS BY FAITH

MORRIS L. VENDEN
LOVE, MARRIAGE, AND RIGHTEOUSNESS BY FAITH

Pacific Press® Publishing Association
Nampa, Idaho
Oshawa, Ontario, Canada

Edited by Lincoln E. Steed
Designed by Tim Larson
Cover photo by Larry Dale Gordon/Image Bank©
Type set in 10/12 Century Schoolbook

The author assumes full responsibility for the accuracy of all facts and quotations cited in this book.

Library of Congress Catalog Card Number: 88-61591

ISBN 0-8163-0784-9

97 98 99 • 6 5 4 3

Contents

Chapter 1
When Two People Meet

This is the last book I ever expected to write! Early in my training to be a pastor, I determined not to talk to anyone about how to have a happy marriage or how to rear the children until I was at least eighty years old.

But I quickly discovered that it is impossible to work as a minister without getting vacuumed into it. Probably 50 percent of the calls a pastor is asked to make have to do with domestic problems.

What goes wrong? Even in this day of easy divorce, it is still true that in most cases, two people who make the decision to marry are hopeful about the outcome. They are attracted to each other and have begun a relationship that has meaning for both of them. Yet approximately one out of every two marriages will end in divorce.

Studying the problems that arise in marriages and in families, I have come to the conclusion that there is one key word for success or failure in a marriage relation, or in any relationship. It is the word *communication*. Communication is the bottom line.

I've been trying to get my wedding sermon down to one word. I haven't tried it publicly yet, although one couple invited me to! I still haven't found the courage. But I have considered, after the candles are lighted, the songs are sung, and they're finally up there, just to shout out one word: "Communication!"

Communication is the basis of the marriage relationship. If

you want to expand it just a little, there must be communication vertically, with God; and communication horizontally, with each other. That's the secret for the successful Christian marriage.

If people would continue to communicate as much after they are married as they did before they were married, there would be a lot more happy homes. It's when the communication breaks down that the trouble begins. So long as communication continues, so does the relationship and so does the love and so does the marriage. If the communication doesn't continue, then neither does the rest of it.

In this volume we will take a closer look at the eight major areas where communication breaks down. We will also notice that these areas of communication are the same ones in which our relationship with God can break down. For the exciting truth is that there is a close similarity between the marriage relationship and the spiritual relationship. The factors that cause us to have a relationship with each other are the same factors that cause us to have a relationship with God; and the same problems that cause breakdown in marriage can also cause a breakdown in the spiritual life.

The eight areas of communication breakdown are: Money, Religion, In-laws, Children, lack of things in Common, Sex, Roles, and Reconciliation. (There's a memory crutch I have used for these—Mr. ICC'S RailRoad!)

But as we consider the various aspects of communication, we will look at each one from two viewpoints—how it relates to marriage and family life, and then how it relates to the Christian life.

Let's start at the very beginning of a marriage relationship. It doesn't begin when two people are standing at the altar, does it? No, it starts when two people meet. And if they like what they see, they begin to communicate with each other.

People don't always like what they see when they first meet. Have you ever had that happen? Have you ever met someone that you didn't care for, but later that person became your best friend, or maybe even your mate?

My roommate in college desperately wanted to get acquainted with a certain young lady on the other side of the campus. He liked what he saw, but she did *not* like what she saw! The attraction was definitely one-sided.

Now it was true that he was not Mr. America. In fact, he had a bigger nose than I did! But I remember him telling me one night, "Oh, if she'll only give me a chance. If only she'll give me a chance. I'm the kind that has to grow on someone—like a wart!"

Well, the interesting thing is that for some reason she did give him a chance, and the day came when I stood up with him at their wedding.

So two people don't always like what they see when they first meet. But if there is any attraction at all, communication can begin, and then a relationship can start. If that relationship continues, love often comes. And when love comes, it can lead to marriage. There is the simple beginning and the evolution of the process two people go through in order to become husband and wife.

There are three elements for communication. In order to become acquainted with someone, you must talk to them. You must listen to them talk to you. You must do things together—work together, travel together, play together. Communication is not always verbal; it also involves shared activities and interests.

We had a church treasurer one time who never said very much. But he had a wife who said it all! One day I stopped by their house, and she was doing her usual thing, and he was doing his. Then he broke in with a surprising remark. He said, "Have you noticed my wife's speech impediment?"

I said, "No, I hadn't noticed."

He said, "She has to stop talking to breathe!"

Before I could reply, his wife said briskly, "Well, at least I don't just sit there and never say anything!"

And he said, "Well, I try not to say anything unless I have something to say."

To which she responded, "That's your problem—it takes you forty-five minutes to *think* of anything to say."

Obviously they had been over this ground before! But so far

as any of us could tell, they were reasonably happy. Apparently the nonverbal communication of going places and doing things together had somehow filled in the gaps for perhaps less than the average amount of verbal communication on the husband's part.

♥　♥　♥

We've taken a few moments on the human side of it, so now let's switch gears and see how it works on the divine side. Two people meet—Christ and the sinner. If they like what they see, communication begins.

Right here we need to ask a question. Do all people like what they see when they meet God? No, they don't! In fact, there has been so much misunderstanding and misapprehension of God that I am convinced God Himself would be insulted if some people were to accept the God they have been told about. It is possible to have such a distorted picture of God that you don't like what you see—and, of course, the devil has worked overtime for centuries to keep that happening.

The average person on planet Earth looks over his glasses toward heaven. When seven people get blown up in a space shuttle, young and old alike can be found looking toward heaven and asking, "Why? Why did God . . . ?" As though God was waiting around up there, looking for some spaceship to blow up, just for fun.

The insurance companies use the same language. Hurricane? Act of God. Tornado? Act of God. Hailstones? God is at work. Earthquakes? Volcanoes? There He goes again! No wonder many people don't like what they see when they are introduced to God.

But even if you have trouble with the concept of God that you have been given by other people, or if you wonder about some of the stories in the Old Testament and what they seem to say about God, let me remind you that the greatest single revelation of God is to be found in the life of Jesus. As you look at Jesus, you are seeing what God is like, what He has always been like, and what He will always be like. You can't help being drawn to Jesus if you take a long look at Him. He is what God is like. If you've seen Him, you've seen God.

But what about God? When God looks at the sinner, does He like what He sees? He sees people who for thousands of years have gone downhill in mental ability, in physical strength, and in moral worth. He sees people who are wretched and miserable and deformed by sin. It is unbelievable that God likes what He sees!

How much easier it would be for God to reach out for fellowship and communion with the angels around His throne who adore him and who are still as He created them. How much easier it would be for Him to wipe out this dark speck in His universe.

We were having an afternoon seminar on one college campus, and a young woman stood up to speak. She said, "This morning I got out of bed and looked up toward the sky and said, 'Good morning, God. Did You have a good night last night?' "

Then she paused and began to think. What kind of a night *did* God have? He looked down on the starving children in Ethiopia. He saw the thousands in Bombay, India, whose only home is the sidewalk: parents, children, and grandparents, all huddled together, trying to sleep. He heard the cries of battered children and weeping widows. He felt the pain of those who tossed and turned in hospital beds. He knew the ache of broken hearts. Being God is not a very pleasant occupation.

When God looks at us, does He like what He sees? His great heart of love is torn apart by our suffering. But He likes *us*. Somehow God is able to see beyond what we are, unloving and unlovable, and He sees what we can become through His grace. He likes what He sees, and He works in every way to reveal Himself to us, so that we will find Him attractive. He continually invites us to give Him a chance. And when that miracle happens, communication between God and man can begin.

At whatever point they decide they like what they see, God and the sinner begin communication. You might have decided you like this God because of a neighbor, friend, teacher, parent, or pastor; for Christianity is caught more than it is taught. You might have decided that you liked what you saw because you opened a book that talked in friendly terms about this God. Maybe you opened your Bible. Somewhere along the line was a starting place, and you said, "I'm interested." Then communication could begin.

How does communication with God take place? Forgive me for giving an elementary-school lesson here. But what must you do in order to communicate with someone? What were the three things we mentioned earlier? In order to communicate, you must talk to someone, you must listen to him talk to you, and you must go places and do things together.

We may not need to be reminded as to how communication takes place in our human relationships. But how easy it is to forget the basics of communication when we transfer it to the Christian life.

I hate to admit how long it took me, even though I was a preacher's kid, to understand this truth. For years I thought that the way to be a Christian was to try hard to be good, and if there was any time left over, read your Bible and pray a little—it'll make God feel good. Only I never had much time left over. I was too exhausted with trying to be good and not making it. That kind of experience will sooner or later drive you to the truth that set Martin Luther on fire. Unless, of course, you find it easy to be good. If the worst thing you have ever done in your life is to chew your fingernails, then you don't need communication with God—or do you?

I'm glad I was bad! I'm glad because "they that be whole need not a physician, but they that are sick." Jesus said, "Go learn what that means." If Jesus directs us to learn what it means, then it must be pretty important.

When you come to the place where you realize that it is not your behavior, but the communication with God, that is the entire basis of the Christian life—just as communication with your mate is the entire basis of marriage—then you can begin to understand the importance of spending time in communication with Him.

We talk to God through prayer. We listen when He talks to us through the study of His Word. We go places and do things together with Him through Christian service and witness and outreach. As we spend time with Him in fellowship and communication and service, the relationship develops. Then it is that love comes and grows and the union of the soul with Christ takes place.

This brings us to a very significant text: "This is the record, that God hath given to us eternal life, and this life is in his Son. He that hath the Son hath life; and he that hath not the Son of God hath not life." 1 John 5:11, 12.

For a long time this text was a mystery to me. It seemed to use the nebulous kind of language for which the Christian church is famous. Many young people have been nothing but frustrated hearing that the way to be a Christian is to "fall on the rock" or to "behold the Lamb" or to "give your heart." These look like yet more intangible phrases. What does it mean here, in John's epistle, to "have the Son"?

Then one day it dawned on me. We use the same kind of language in speaking of our human relationships. We say, "I have a wife"; "You have a husband"; "I have a friend." We simply mean we have a relationship with that person. We have communication with that person. We know that person. So if I have Jesus, the Son of God, I have a relationship with Him. And if I have a relationship with Him, I have life—now. That's good news!

The apostle John is famous for that good news. Sit down sometime and read through his gospel and underline all the verses where we are promised that we can have life now. It's not something that we're going to receive later. We can have it now. Here is the basis for certainty of eternal life. If I have a relationship with God, if the communication in that relationship continues, then the love will continue, and the place at the marriage supper of the Lamb is assured. "This is life eternal, that they might know thee the only true God, and Jesus Christ, whom thou hast sent." John 17:3.

My wife and I were standing in the airport in Tokyo, on our way to Seoul, Korea. In the line at the ticket counter we met a young man from Sweden who was also on his way to Seoul, to get married. The marriage was to be held that very week—but he had not yet met her! He was looking forward to meeting her, but they had never yet met personally. They had been writing letters, exchanging photographs, and had decided to become man and wife, even though they had never met. He was anxious to meet her. We were anxious for him!

Two people who learn to love each other want to be together, personally and for keeps. If you would like to try a definition for marriage, even in this present day, how would that one do? Marriage is when two people who love each other get together—personally and permanently.

We live in a world of uncertainty. Even once the marriage vows are spoken, there can be uncertainty. People end up sitting on their nerves, wondering, "Could there ever be . . . ?" "Will we continue, or will we . . . ?" "Might it ever happen that . . . ?"

But when we enter into the relationship with God—the eternal life that begins here and now through fellowship with Him—there is no uncertainty. There is a lonely cross that stands as positive assurance that we are invited into the presence of God and that He will never change His mind concerning us.

Jesus wants to get married! His is one proposal of marriage that is offered to every human being. No one needs to live life alone. Not one is forced to remain single. Jesus wants to get married. You can read about it in Revelation 19:6-8. "I heard as it were the voice of a great multitude, and as the voice of many waters, and as the voice of mighty thunderings, saying, Alleluia: for the Lord God omnipotent reigneth. Let us be glad and rejoice, and give honour to him: for the marriage of the Lamb is come, and his wife hath made herself ready. And to her was granted that she should be arrayed in fine linen, clean and white: for the fine linen is the righteousness of saints."

Jesus wants to get married. And if we accept of His love and begin the relationship and communion with Him, our union that begins here will last forever—and "forever is a long, long time."

Chapter 2
Crazy About Money

A survey was taken of 700 couples in the Midwest whose marriage was no more, and it was discovered that 70 percent attributed their major problem to economic factors. Money. In our society it is impossible to live without it. Every society has some medium of exchange, whether it is dollars and cents or beads or jewelry or cattle or some other valued items. But in our culture today, money plays an important role.

Perhaps the greatest single problem with money is that of indebtedness. In America today, we don't need money anymore. All we need is a little piece of plastic. It comes in a variety of colors and opens the door for all kinds of purchases—until the end of the month. Then you discover that you need money after all, right? No wonder someone said, "What our family needs is plastic surgery!"

The pressure of debt can be a major contributor to the breakdown of communication in marriage. When they run into financial problems, she blames him for the difficulty, and he blames her. The accusations continue until love wanes, and the entire relationship is in trouble—not just the family finances!

One wonderful day in our own home we put all of our credit cards on a dish, there in the family room, and lighted a match to them. We watched the smoke go toward heaven like sweet incense! But that wasn't the end of it. It was another three years before we were able to finish making all the payments for the spending that those cards represented.

The willingness of the pioneers to sit on apple boxes until

15

they could afford to pay cash on the barrelhead seems to have been replaced by an impatience to have everything *now*. We are no longer interested in following in the footsteps of Grandpa, who walked twenty miles to school in the snow—and came home for lunch! But having the luxuries of life on the installment plan has often been a curse rather than a blessing.

Jesus had something to say about the problem in Luke 12. He told a story about a small barn and a big fool. But He began the parable by giving the warning, "Take heed, and beware of covetousness: for a man's life consisteth not in the abundance of the things which he possesseth." Verse 15. The King James Version makes it into almost a tongue twister, doesn't it? But today, in the time of equal rights for women, let's include them in the picture. "Take heed, and beware of covetousness: for a woman's life consisteth not in the abundance of the things which she possesseth." If we were to give heed to these words from Jesus, perhaps there would be a lot less stress on the financial front. If married couples remembered this counsel, many problems would be averted.

There are, of course, many other money areas that can cause a breakdown in communication. For instance, who manages the money? Is it the husband's job, or the wife's? Or does each person manage his own area of the financial picture?

No matter who is supposed to be in charge of managing the money, there should be agreement on how the money is to be managed. Does each have the same priorities when it comes to deciding what is necessity, what is luxury, what should be spent, what should be saved?

Back in the pioneer days, there were very few necessities—I read a report which listed five, one of which was soap. Today the list of necessities includes more than 100 items, one of which is color TV! So there can be big differences when it comes to deciding what is necessity and what isn't.

Then there are the problems that have come as a result of two checks coming into the household. Sometimes one partner is inclined to say, "What's yours is mine, and what's mine is mine." How do you relate to this in your household? Are all funds pooled, or does each one take responsibility for certain expenses? People have gotten at each other's throats over this modern-day dilemma.

Then there is the area of independent spending, where either the husband or wife feels free to go out and spend a certain amount of money without consulting the other. When the mate learns of this expenditure, it's nothing but "Pass the salt" for three days. It can be a good idea to sit down by the fire in some of your quiet moments, with your feet on the hassock, with the popcorn and the apples, and discuss this one. Are you free to spend $5, or $20, or $100 without consensus?

What about tithes and offerings? What happens when one wants to pay tithes and offerings, and the other one doesn't? Is the tithe paid first, right off the top, or do you wait until the other bills are paid and see how much is left over? Homes have been divided on the question of tithes and offerings.

I always feel sorry for the people who decide that they cannot afford to pay tithe; in fact, one of the reasons they aren't able to afford it is that they don't pay it! The Bible axiom is that $9 with God's blessing goes much further than $10 without His blessing. You can read about it in Malachi Chapter 3. It's the only place in the Bible where God invites us to try Him out, to prove Him, to put Him on trial. And if you make the decision not to return the tithes and offerings to Him, you are always the loser. But not everyone has the same background and understanding in this area, and there can come a real breakdown of communication when one person has a conviction on the subject of tithes and offerings that is not shared by his mate.

Well, what do you do when you see a breakdown of communication in the realm of money and finance? The only thing to do is to communicate! If your relationship is suffering a lack of communication on money matters, then the answer is to deliberately set aside time to try to communicate with each other about the issues on which you disagree. It would be wise to discuss as much as possible premarriage to discover the areas of common ideas and values on financial issues. But if it needs to happen postmarriage, as well, then it is still important to communicate and try to work out a compromise.

Now I'd like to share with you something that comes from a book entitled *Money Madness,* by Goldberg and Lewis.

They point out that we either duplicate or we rebel against our childhood experiences concerning money. If we were brought up poor, we are going to have a certain mind-set concerning money in the future. If we were brought up wealthy, the same thing. And we will often either do the same thing as our parents, or we will rebel and do the opposite.

Some of us have experienced this pattern on many levels of lifestyle and habits, not just as it relates to money.

My father always locked the car wherever we went. It seemed like even when we stopped at the mailbox along the street to mail a letter, we'd get out, lock the car, try the doors, try the trunk, mail the letter, go back, unlock the car, and get back into the car. When a kid is anxious to get to the fireworks that have already started, that is more than a kid can take, to have to wait to lock the car and check the trunk!

So today, I leave the keys in the car, sometimes with the motor running, as a rebellion against this!

We accept or react to our upbringing on the economic level as well. Our own temperaments can also lead us to certain reactions when it comes to the managing of money.

The book *Money Madness* lists four categories where most people fall concerning money.

1. Money as security
2. Money as freedom
3. Money as love
4. Money as power

Let's go back and explain each one of these just briefly.

Money as security. Here is a person who feels that the more money he can save and stash away and build up in the bank, the greater is his security. The more he has put away, the better he feels. So he is tight with his money. His savings account is extremely important to him. He probably still has the first nickel he ever made! Money for him is a method of security.

Money as freedom. This person has perhaps been a slave to something or someone in the past because of lack of money. He wants complete independence, and if he can have and manage his own money, he doesn't have to answer to anyone. For him, money is of value as a ticket to freedom.

Money as love. Here is the person who sees money as a method for expressing love and purchasing love. He buys expensive gifts, that he may not be able to afford. He throws fancy parties. He uses his money to buy acceptance and approval; and he can also use it for the opposite goal. If he wants to reject someone, he will withhold the gifts, as a method of expressing disapproval.

Money as power. For this person, money has become a tool to manipulate those around him. He sees money as political power, a tool to influence those in high places and induce them to certain decisions or behaviors. This type of person will often live beyond his means, to give the illusion of greater wealth than he actually possesses. The intent is to gain control over those around him.

Well, we may not be able to help our particular temperaments and backgrounds. However, it can help to understand ourselves a little better, when some of the marital disagreements come. Suppose a person who sees money as security, and wants to save every penny, marries someone who sees money as love, and wants to be showered with gifts and luxuries in order to feel genuinely accepted. There are going to be problems right at the outset, aren't there?

What do you do about it? You talk about it! Ideally, you talk about it before you marry. But when problems surface after the marriage, you talk about it then. Communication is the answer to the breakdown of communication. *Communication* is always the key word.

♥ ♥ ♥

Missing from the Goldberg and Lewis treatise is a fifth category for the Christian. The Christian does not talk and think only in terms of self and his own freedom or security or need for love and acceptance or desire for controlling others. The spirit of Jesus gives the Christian a center and focus on the needs of others, that those who operate according to the world's standard do not recognize or experience. The fifth category for the purpose and use of money is to see money as *service*.

When you see money from a Christian perspective, as a means for service, there may be an overlap into the other areas. For instance, you may want to save as much as possible, so that you will be in a position to help as many as possible—saving that you may give. Or you may give freely to those who are in need, because you have experienced the love of Christ for a lost world—instead of merely giving to those who are your special friends. When money becomes primarily a tool for service and outreach and ministry to others, the human insanity on the subject of money gives way to Christian sanity.

The person who has looked at money for security can read 1 Timothy 6:17. "Charge them that are rich in this world, that they be not highminded, nor trust in uncertain riches, but in the living God, who giveth us richly all things to enjoy." One who has discovered money as service no longer finds his security in money. Instead, he puts his trust in the living God.

The person who has looked at money as freedom can read 2 Peter 2:19. Peter is talking about Balaam, who had a money-madness problem. It says so in verse 16: He "was rebuked for his iniquity: the dumb ass speaking with man's voice forbad the madness of the prophet." Balaam was a victim of money madness. But notice verse 19. "Of whom a man is overcome, of the same is he brought in bondage." If I am looking to money for freedom, according to the Bible, then, like Balaam I am going to end up in bondage. True freedom comes from Christ and the gift He offers. And if the Son shall make you free, ye shall be free indeed.

The person who has looked at money as love can go to the Song of Solomon 8:7. "Many waters cannot quench love, neither can the floods drown it." And then it says, "If a man would give all the substance of his house for love, it would utterly be contemned." The New International Version says, "If one were to give all the wealth of his house for love, it would be utterly scorned." You cannot buy love with money. You might buy attention or temporary companionship. But you cannot buy love. And many waters cannot quench love, even if there is a lack of money.

Finally, for the person who has looked at money as a method for control, have a look at Matthew 20:25-28. The disciples were angry because they were worried about who was going to be the greatest. They had been trying to arrange things so they could get ahead of the next person. But Jesus knew their hearts, and He had something to say to them. "Jesus called them unto him, and said, Ye know that the princes of the Gentiles exercise dominion over them, and they that are great exercise authority upon them. But it shall not be so among you: But whosoever will be great among you, let him be your minister; and whosoever will be chief among you, let him be your servant: even as the Son of man came not to be ministered unto, but to minister, and to give his life a ransom for many." Verse 25.

The Christian does not need to be in control of others, because as Jesus said, he is more interested in being a servant than a master.

So if I don't need to use my money for control, if I don't need to use money to buy love, if I don't have to use it to get freedom or hoard it for my own security, then I can use it in service for others.

Jesus is the great Example of this. "Ye know the grace of our Lord Jesus Christ, that, though he was rich, yet for your sakes he became poor, that ye through his poverty might be rich." 2 Corinthians 8:9. Jesus, the richest in the universe, who owned the cattle on a thousand hills, as well as extensive mining assets, who was worshiped by all the angels and the unfallen worlds left all of that and became poor. How poor? So poor that He had no place to lay His head. So poor that He went from His birth in a stable, to sleeping along with His disciples in the open air and on the ground, to being buried in a borrowed tomb. He became the poorest of the poor, that we, through His poverty, might be made rich. When we become partakers of His Spirit, we will not only gladly use our money and resources in service for Him, but we will be doing it from the right motives.

It is possible to bring our tithes and offerings to God, and even to engage in service for Him, from selfish motives, isn't it? For instance, if I am using money for security, but I understand the theory of Christian stewardship, I may bring my tithes and offerings to the church as a sort of insurance. If I pay my tithe, then the grasshoppers will stop at my fence, right? They may eat my neighbor's crops, but they won't eat mine!

That's why I like the story about the man who had been faithful in his tithes and offerings, and who had gone even further than that and dedicated his lands and possessions to the Lord. And his neighbors knew it.

The grasshoppers came, and they ate his neighbor's crops, and then they jumped the fence and ate his crops too.

The neighbors came and scoffed, and said, "What do you have to say now?"

The man replied, "If the good Lord wants to graze His grasshoppers on His own land, that's His business. Meanwhile, I will love and trust Him regardless."

But if I am giving my gifts to the Lord primarily in order to gain security for myself, I will be sadly disappointed if things don't turn out the way I expect.

If my motives are selfish and I see money in terms of freedom, then I may bring my tithes and offerings to God in order to buy freedom. If I give God my 10 percent, then I think I will be free to use my 90 percent as I please. But the truth is, how much of it is His? All of it! All that we have and are belongs to Him.

If I see money as a method to buy love, I may bring my tithes and offerings to try and buy God's love. There is a Bible story about a man who tried to do just that. Simon wanted to buy God's power with money, but Peter said to him, "Thy money perish with thee, because thou hast thought that the gift of God may be purchased with money." Acts 8:20. What is the gift of God? It includes His love. "God so loved the world that He gave." So no wonder Peter told this poor man, "Thou hast neither part nor lot in this matter: for thy heart is not right in the sight of God. Repent therefore of this thy wickedness, and pray God, if perhaps the thought of thine heart may be forgiven thee. For I perceive that thou art in the gall of bitterness, and in the bond of iniquity." Verses 21-23.

There is nothing we can do to earn or merit God's gifts, and the person who tries to buy God's gifts, whether His love or His power or His salvation or any other of His gifts, is in the gall of bitterness and in the bond of iniquity.

Finally, you have the person who wants to use money as power, even when it comes to bringing tithes and offerings. Such people seize on God's carte blanche in Malachi 3, where He says, "Prove me now." Such pay their tithes and offerings in order to put God under obligation to open the windows of heaven and pour out a blessing. Yet God will not allow Himself to be put in a corner, if you please. True, the promise of His blessing given in Malachi 3 is not contingent upon our motives being right. Yet it is still His goal for each of His children that we grow to the right motives and seek to further His work by using our funds in service with Him.

That's the fifth alternative again. Money is intended for service. "Thus saith the Lord, Let not the wise man glory in his wisdom, neither let the mighty man glory in his might, let not the rich man glory in his riches: but let him that glorieth glory in this, that he understandeth and knoweth me, that I am the Lord which exercise lovingkindness." Jeremiah 9:23, 24. That's the one thing where all your security and your freedom and your love reside—in your personal relationship with Jesus Christ.

Money itself is of no more value than sand, except as it is used to relieve the necessities of life, to be a blessing to others, and to advance the cause of Christ.

The story is told of a couple who contracted to fly many thousands of dollars in cash in a private plane from a remote area to the bank in the city. Expecting the flight to take just a few hours, they took off on their assignment with hundreds of thousands of dollars in steel boxes behind the seats.

But they ran into bad weather and were forced to make an emergency landing out in the middle of nowhere. Even though they were carrying such a large amount of money, they discovered something important. No matter how much money you have, you can't eat it, you can't use it for medical help, you can't use it to keep warm, you can't sleep on it, and you can't escape with it. They discovered the truth that money is of no value in and of itself—it is of no more value than sand.

No wonder the Scriptures are so clear, in the appeal of Jesus from long ago, "Lay not up for yourselves treasures upon earth, where moth and rust doth corrupt, and where thieves break through and steal: but lay up for yourselves treasures in heaven, where neither moth nor rust doth corrupt, and where thieves do not break through nor steal: for where your treasure is, there will your heart be also." Matthew 6:19-21.

If we do not share God's priorities when it comes to money, there will be a breakdown of communication in our relationship with Him. This happened to the rich young ruler, as recorded in Matthew 19. When he learned how God looked at money, he went away sorrowful, because his interest in his possessions was greater than his interest in the kingdom of heaven.

You may not be rich in silver and gold, but you might be rich in intelligence or talent or good looks or backbone. Whatever your riches are, if you depend upon those riches instead of depending upon God, there will be a breakdown in your communion and relationship with Him. Wherever your treasure is, there will your heart be also.

It almost sounds backward, doesn't it? Shouldn't Jesus have said, "Where your heart is, there will your treasure be also?" Let's try for an illustration. When the stock market crashes, who is the most concerned: those who have invested money in the stock market, or those who haven't? The answer is obvious, isn't it? In the same way, when we have invested our talents and our means in the cause of God, we have a vital interest in His work that cannot be shared by those who have not made such an investment.

Lay not up for yourselves treasure on earth. Don't depend upon your earthly treasure that you do have, no matter in what form it may be. If your dependence is upon God, and all your treasures are brought to Him in loving service, He will have your heart. For where your treasure is, there will your heart be also.

Chapter 3
Being Spiritual Versus Being Religious

We had kept in touch with their family for years. The two daughters my wife and I had sort of "raised from puppies" came by for a visit on their way home from the university. Both of the young women were now close to six feet tall, and they confided in us that throughout all of their high school and college years they had never even had a date, let alone a serious romantic relationship.

They weren't particularly interested in living alone for the rest of their lives, but they weren't finding it easy to meet eligible partners. So my wife and I tried to do the usual thing and convince them that there are worse things than not being married. But our arguments were cheap and not very impressive or convincing, even in our eyes.

Our friends went their way. Surprisingly, within a year, both of them were married.

The first sister found one who seemed to be the perfect match. He was tall, good-looking, and a member of the same church she was. He seemed very dedicated to the church, but shortly after the marriage, she began to see evidence that his commitment to God was only external. The marriage didn't last long, and she ended up alone, wondering about a God who had allowed her so much unhappiness and disappointment.

The second sister met a man who seemed to love God, but who was not a member of her church. She went through a real struggle, trying to decide whether or not she should marry him. Finally she went ahead and they were married. Within just a year or two, he joined her church.

There is Bible counsel on the subject, found in 2 Corinthians 6:14, 15, "Be ye not unequally yoked together with unbelievers: for what fellowship hath righteousness with unrighteousness? and what communion hath light with darkness? and what concord hath Christ with Belial? or what part hath he that believeth with an infidel?" Even secular counselors will advise against marriage to one who does not share your religious beliefs and priorities. But we have sometimes had a very surface definition of what makes a believer and what makes an unbeliever. We have concluded that a believer is anyone who belongs to my own particular church, and anyone who does not belong to my church must be an unbeliever. That's not necessarily so. It's not that simple, as many have learned to their sorrow.

There can be a vast difference between being spiritual and being only religious. Even two atheists may find sufficient common ground to be compatible, both comfortable in their unbelief. And two spiritual people can find unity and harmony. But if two people marry, even if they belong to the same denomination, and one is spiritual while the other has only external religious interest, there will be constant friction and pressure.

We pondered the situation of the two sisters and their marriages and wondered about the second sister and her positive result. Then one year the second sister and her husband and daughter came to our home for a visit, and I had the opportunity to quiz her.

"Would you do it over again? Would you go ahead and marry someone not of your church, so long as he shared your love for God?"

Without hesitation she replied, "No, I wouldn't."

I was surprised. I hadn't expected that answer. In fact, I tried to talk her out of it. But she insisted.

She said, "No, it's too risky. I've compared notes with my friends. I took a great chance in going against the Bible counsel on the subject. It would have been far better if I had waited. But God has been very good to me."

So the principle still applies. When two people have differing religious beliefs, even when both of them love God, there can be breakdowns in communication. But if only doctrinal unity is present, without spiritual unity, the risks are even greater.

Contrary to what we would like to think, religion is not only the great healer, it can be the great divider. It seems ironic, but the One known as the Prince of Peace said, "I came not to send peace, but a sword." Matthew 10:34.

Within every church there are those who know God, and those who don't know God. Within every denomination there are those who are spiritual, and those who are only religious.

One day I went to call on an older woman, well into her eighties. She seemed to be one of the pillars of the church, and at first I thought this visit was only routine. At the end of the conversation, I asked her, "Is there anything that I, as your pastor, can do for you?"

She said, "Yes. Would you please help me get out of this religion? I go through the motions. I go to church. I go to prayer meeting. I can't help it. It's a habit. But I hate it. I would give anything to be able to get away from it." And she pleaded with me to help her escape from the church of which I was the pastor!

Well, I hastened to assure her that this was not part of my job description. She was an extreme example of someone who was a victim of being religious, without ever having understood what it meant to be spiritual.

The religious person is often a second- third- or fourth-generation church member. The religious person knows all the rules and regulations, all the standards, all the doctrines of the church. He goes through the motions, but he has beaten such a hard path from his house to the door of the church that there's scarcely a crack in which the seed of the gospel can take root.

One woman said, "When my parents joined the church, years ago, it was because of two things. One, they had a great need, experienced the new birth, and found a deep relationship with God. Two, they had an understanding of the doctrines and beliefs of the church and joined to fellowship with those who shared those beliefs.

"My brothers and sisters and I were raised to understand the doctrinal part of their religion and accepted it intellectually. But somehow we never seemed to experience the relationship with God that my parents knew. We only went through the forms and the routine, because we believed it was 'right' as far as doctrine was concerned.

"Now our children, in spite of their instruction in doctrine, have thrown out the whole package and have no connection with God or the church."

Perhaps one of the greatest reasons for the large numbers leaving organized religion today is that they understand only the facts, but never experience the *"faith* of our fathers" for themselves. The person who knows only a legalistic religion, who understands being religious, but has never known what it means to be spiritual, finds it easy to go away from even the religious routine in the end.

On the other hand, the person who is spiritual is one who has an ongoing, meaningful relationship with the Lord Jesus. Conversion is the beginning of that experience. But the spiritual know not only the rules and standards and doctrines, they also know the Lord. Jesus is the center and focus of their lives. There is no such thing for the spiritual person as going out the door in the morning and saying, "Oh, I forgot my devotions!" The whole focus and priority of the life is the time with God, the communication with Him, that is the entire basis of the Christian life. For the spiritual person, the private life with God runs competition with nothing else, and nothing else runs competition with it. The spiritual person loves to spend time where the things of God, faith, heaven, and eternity are being discussed.

An unconverted person may find it easy to discuss religious topics, and even use the discussion as an escape from considering the matters of the heart. Almost every church or institution or college campus has a group who love to discuss the intellectual things connected with religion. They discuss such topics as whether or not God knows the future, how long eternity really is, or what angels' wings are made of. There is intellectual stimulation and enthusiastic discussion, with one mind sparring against another. But the name of Jesus is conspicuously absent.

As you may know, there are three kinds of communication. First, there's mouth-to-mouth—and that's not what some young people might think! Mouth-to-mouth communication is chitchat. Small talk. "Hi." "How are you doing?" "Fine." "See you later." Chitchat.

The second kind of communication is head-to-head. It's the intellectual exchange. "What do you think about the Middle East?" "Whom do you think should win the election?" "What do you think about the unemployment problem?" Some have called it "head-tripping," and you can head-trip about any number of topics, even religious ones.

The third kind of communication is heart-to-heart. In heart-to-heart communication, you not only talk about what you think, but you share how you feel. You share spiritual goals and insights; you talk about Jesus and what He's done for you, personally. Many in the Christian church have yet to understand heart-to-heart communication. Many homes do not know of it. Heart-to-heart communication is rare. But it is the deepest form of communication.

Those who are only religious may become involved in religious discussions on the head-to-head level. But only the spiritual can know the meaning of the heart-to-heart sharing that is available to the genuine Christian.

But the condition of the majority of the Christian church today is to be religious without being spiritual. That's why the church of today is called Laodicea. *Laodicea* means "lukewarm." In order for a church to be called lukewarm, more than 50 percent of its members must be lukewarm, or the church would have been called something else instead.

You can read about the Laodicean church in Revelation Chapter 3. It gives a description of the three groups of people that exist until just shortly before Jesus comes again. There are the hot, the cold, and the lukewarm—with the lukewarm being in the majority.

Notice verse 14 and onward. "Unto the angel of the church of the Laodiceans write; These things saith the Amen, the faithful and true witness, the beginning of the creation of God; I know thy works, that thou art neither cold nor hot: I would thou wert cold or hot." So God prefers even cold to lukewarm! "So then because thou art lukewarm, and neither cold nor hot, I will spew thee out of my mouth." God is saying here, "Lukewarm makes me sick!" That's a pretty strong statement, isn't it?

But what *is* lukewarm? In order to get lukewarm water in the kitchen, you turn on both faucets, equal parts of hot and cold, right? Usually the hot is on the left and the cold is on the right. I took a shower in a foreign country one day where it was just the opposite, and I did some kind of weird rain dance before I finally found out which was which! But if you turn on equal parts of hot and cold, you get lukewarm. That's a basic lesson in home economics!

When God calls people lukewarm, He is obviously not talking about people who are hot on the left side and cold on the right side. That wouldn't make sense. But if you go to Matthew 23, you find the description of people who are a mixture of hot and cold—they are hot on the outside, but cold on the inside. And that fits.

Jesus called these people "whited sepulchres." Matthew 23:27. They looked good on the outside, but inside they were rotten. They did all of the right things for all of the wrong reasons. So they were lukewarm, being a combination of hot and cold. The Laodicean church is so often hot on works, but cold on faith and love and the Holy Spirit. That's what makes Laodicea lukewarm.

Well, what happens to these lukewarm people in Revelation 3? There is no lukewarm reward for the lukewarm, when Jesus comes again! In all of the descriptions of the end time, only two groups are mentioned. They are called various names: the sheep and the goats, the wheat and the tares, the righteous and the wicked, the just and the unjust. But just two groups—the third middle group has disappeared. They have gone one way or the other. And it is happening today. It is one of the greatest evidences of the fact that the coming of Jesus is right upon us.

Many homes, churches, and institutions are becoming painfully aware that while you may have had unity for years as lukewarm people gathered warmth from the lukewarm people around them, the unity disappears as they begin going one way or the other. Two lukewarm people may live together in harmony for years, but when there is a sudden change and one goes hot and the other goes cold, the two are unequally yoked together and the problems begin. We are seeing it happen all around us today, and it will crescendo as we draw closer to the return of Christ. Perhaps this is one of the greatest reasons why the Christian church has almost matched the world's statistics for divorce.

What do you do if you find yourself in this situation? There's some counsel for you in 1 Corinthians 7. It says for the believer to stay by until and unless the unbeliever chooses to go. It is the unbeliever who will often choose to leave, because unbelievers are uncomfortable in the presence of believers. But in the meantime, you go to your knees for the grace to maintain your integrity and your trust in God.

What is it that changes the lukewarm from their middle-of-the-road, fence-straddling position? Look in Revelation 3:18-21 and notice the counsel of the True Witness. "I counsel thee to buy of me gold tried in the fire, that thou mayest be rich; and white raiment, that thou mayest be clothed, and that the shame of thy nakedness do not appear; and anoint thine eyes with eyesalve, that thou mayest see. As many as I love, I rebuke and chasten: be zealous therefore, and repent. Behold, I stand at the door, and knock: if any man hear my voice, and open the door, I will come in to him, and will sup with him, and he with me. To him that overcometh will I grant to sit with me in my throne, even as I also overcame, and am set down with my Father in his throne."

As you study the symbolism of Bible prophecy, you will discover that gold represents faith and love, white raiment represents the righteousness of Christ, and the eye salve represents the insight brought by the Holy Spirit. As the counsel of the True Witness is heeded, the lukewarm majority disappear. People are brought to decision by the presentation of a mes-

sage of the need for faith and love and the righteousness of
Christ and the Holy Spirit. Those who follow the counsel become hot, while those who refuse become cold. Those who accept the counsel open the door to the One who stands knocking for admission. They begin to fellowship with Him day by
day, through His word and through prayer. They accept His
discipline without losing their trust in His love, because they
know Him personally. By beholding Him, they are changed
into His image, becoming overcomers through the power from
above them, even as He also overcame through dependence
upon His Father.

As the message of Jesus and His righteousness is uplifted,
the lukewarm go one way or the other. When Jesus preached
His message of self-surrender, the whole nation was divided.
Those who were satisfied with their own righteousness ended
up crucifying Him, while those who accepted His righteousness were willing to follow Him, even unto the death.

The apostle Paul preached Jesus and Him crucified, and
wherever he went, there was either a revival or a riot. Nobody
ever stayed the same. No one can stay the same today when
that message of Jesus and His righteousness is presented.

I'm going to predict that you know which way you are going
today. You probably have an idea which way your mate, and
perhaps the rest of your family and friends, is going. The great
divide is taking place, and everyone, everywhere, both inside
and outside the church, is either becoming more and more interested in God and the gospel of Christ, or less and less interested. It's happening in the world; it's happening in the
church. Before long, every person will have made the decision
that will determine his eternal destiny.

What are you deciding in your own heart? The door of
probation is still open today, and nothing can prevent you
from accepting of the salvation that is offered, except your
own stubborn choice.

For the sake of the One who stands knocking, won't you
open the door? Invite Him to come in to fellowship with you,
not only today, but every day until you see Him face to face.

Chapter 4
It's All in the Family

"I have a proposal to make. I am asking you to be my wife. However, there are certain qualifications. First, I wish it understood that I love my mother more than I do you. This is understandable, I am sure, when you consider that I have known her so much longer than I have you.

"Second, if it comes to a crisis with respect to any basic decision, of course I will consult my father rather than you. You are still young and inexperienced, whereas my father is older and very wise. He is the head of a business in which I wish to make a name for myself, so you can understand how I feel.

"Third, I am reserving my room with my parents, because I plan to spend most of my time in their home. Our family is very close, and I feel I should preserve the family unity as it has been in the past. My nine brothers and sisters mean much to me, and I'm sure you will not mind if I spend most of my time with my family. I hope you will not mind staying alone.

"Fourth, a word about my property. You must understand that it belongs to me exclusively. If you accept my proposal, I shall want you to sign legal documents making no claims on my property or money. I find it hard to say goodbye to my money. I am sure a clever girl like you will be able to find a job that will support you.

"Oh yes—another thing. I cannot bear sickness, tears, or sorrow. So please do not expect me, when we are married, to give you any sympathy and attention. I need my sleep and will not want to be bothered with your problems. Bear your own

33

crosses, and keep your chin up.

"I do want you to be my wife, and as such you will have the full responsibility for our children, the meals, and all household duties, so that I shall be free to give my full attention to my mother, father, brothers and sisters, my possessions, and my business.

"You are a nice girl, and I feel sure we could have some good times together. Will you say Yes? If you do, I shall go and ask my mother if it is all right. If there is a wedding, your family will stand the expense."*

This satire is an exaggerated statement of the involvement of the in-laws and their potential for causing a breakdown of communication in marriage. But in a more subtle sense, it has been true to life in many cases. Most of us are familiar with the fact that the relatives can cause real problems in a marriage—and the jokes about the in-laws, particularly the mother-in-law stories, are numberless.

Jesus had something to say that is right to the point, in Matthew 19:4, 5. "He answered and said unto them, Have ye not read, that he which made them at the beginning made them male and female, and said, For this cause shall a man leave father and mother, and shall cleave to his wife: and they twain shall be one flesh?" In this day of equal rights and responsibility, let's rephrase it. "For this cause shall a woman leave father and mother." And, we might add, "for this cause shall father and mother *let* them leave!" That would have to be included as well, wouldn't it?

Two key words here: *leave* and *cleave*. In order for the second to take place, the first is essential. If you want the Bible counsel on the subject, there it is. If you're going to follow the Bible on the subject, then you clip the strings. How fortunate are the young people whose parents are willing to have that happen. There are some parents who aren't.

An elder of one church was a bachelor of more than forty years. His mother had needed him too much for him to ever be

---

*Written by Arthur L. Bietz.

free to marry. She needed him so badly that she became an invalid in order to keep him. She was bedridden, and so of course he had to stay single and live at home in order to take care of her needs.

One night, one of the church members dropped by the house unexpectedly, and the shade at the door was open just a crack. When they knocked on the door, they saw her *run* across the room and hop back into bed!

Well, hers was a particularly tragic case, but there are many more modified versions that are just as deadly. The Bible counsel remains: In order to follow the plan of God in marriage and the formation of a new home, you are to leave father and mother, and cleave to your mate.

What does it mean to leave father and mother? It doesn't mean to leave your honor and respect for your parents, for the fifth commandment instructs us to honor them. So if you were to leave your honor and respect for your parents, you would be breaking one of the commandments. You don't leave your love for your parents when you marry. But there is one thing that you do leave—you leave your dependence on father and mother. That's the one essential thing to leave.

Marriage is for grown-ups. If you are unready to leave your dependence upon your parents, whether it is emotional dependence or financial dependence or any other kind, then you are not old enough to get married!

Happy is the couple who do not depend upon their parents financially, although sometimes you can get away with it while finishing school, so you can eat something more than peanut-butter sandwiches. But there can still be problems in some cases, because of strings attached to any financial assistance. However, the Bible instruction is clear. If two young people discover that they have greater-than-average potential for problems with the in-laws, the best thing they can do is move to the other side of the country for the first few years until they have plowed their own furrow for a while. Then sometimes the closeness can work out peacefully later in the marriage.

Emotional dependence is probably even more crippling than financial dependence, and it can come in many different ways.

Perhaps a parent thinks, "No one is good enough for our daughter." Prince Charming himself could come along, and they would not be impressed! This kind of thinking can carry over into the relationship with the new mate. He wasn't good enough, he still isn't good enough, and he never will be.

Then you have the problem of overattachment. Often this happens in a single-parent home or in a home where the parents' marriage has been unhappy. The parent has substituted the relationship with a son or daughter for that which he lacked in his own marriage, and there is real stress when the time comes to leave father and mother. Suddenly the parent is being replaced, and he will fight with everything he has to keep this from happening.

Some young people faced with the problem of a domineering parent have never learned to make decisions for themselves. This crippling dependency carries over into the marriage, and the conflicts begin in earnest. It is a solemn fact that when you marry, you not only pledge to love the one you've chosen, but you also pledge to love the ones that he loves as well. But there can be personality conflicts when the domineering parent continues to try to call the shots after the marriage has begun.

We do have different personalities and different ways, and it is inevitable that we will be closer to some people than to others. When you consider the difficulties that two people can have in trying to blend their personalities and harmonize their differences, it is no wonder that the problem is compounded when you add in the varying temperaments of a dozen or two relatives and in-laws!

Again, particularly in the beginning years of marriage, geographical distance is sometimes the best solution. It will allow the couple time and privacy to work out their life together without interference. But whatever steps need to be taken, the basic Bible principle always applies: we are to leave father and mother.

There seem to be two peak times during marriage when problems with the relatives are most critical. The first, as we have noticed, is the early years of adjustment. The second stage of adjustment comes late in life, when the parents are aging and dependent.

People need to be treated with great understanding as they grow older, don't they? All of us have certain little traits that are peculiar to our personalities. Our friends and family know what these are. If you are particularly neat and orderly, your friends know it. If you tend to be a hypochondriac, your family has noticed. If you are absent-minded or a procrastinator or stubborn, or talkative or generous, you can't have kept it a secret! And as you grow older, the traits you are known for will become more pronounced. Something novel and interesting in someone at age forty might be the thing that will kill them at age ninety, because we tend to become more like we are than what we were!

As we approach the later years in our relationships with parents and relatives, it is important to remember the better days. To remember what has gone before can be a big help in dealing with today's frustrations. The time will come when we will wish for the same courtesy for ourselves.

It can be helpful to try to look upon the relationship with the relatives as a friendship, whether in later life, as parents have grown old and the roles are reversed, or at the beginning of marriage, when the children first begin their own home. When you have friends, you may solicit advice, and they may offer their advice for what it's worth. But no one has authority to insist that their advice be carried out.

My father loves to give advice! It was refreshing to go back home after my marriage, and to be able for the first time to take the advice, or leave it, as I chose—including what to eat! "Sorry, Dad, but I don't have to eat my spinach anymore! I'm married now. I'm an adult. No thanks, I wouldn't care for any!"

Parents, if you can keep yourselves from it, don't give advice until it's asked for! But children, don't forget to ask for advice. You may need it. Any fool can learn by his own hard experience. It takes a wise person to learn from the experience of others.

♥　♥　♥

Now let's shift gears and notice the factors from which we

gain spiritual insight concerning our marriage to Christ.

Earlier we noticed Jesus' strange statement in Matthew 10:34. "Think not that I am come to send peace on earth: I came not to send peace, but a sword." Who was He talking to? Families? Relatives? Let's continue: "For I am come to set a man at variance against his father, and the daughter against her mother, and the daughter-in-law against her mother-in-law. And a man's foes shall be they of his own household. He that loveth father or mother more than me is not worthy of me: And he that loveth son or daughter more than me is not worthy of me." Verses 35-37.

Those are hard-hitting words, aren't they? Jesus made some strong demands in terms of commitment. No one is to be more important to us than Jesus Himself. No one, not even father or mother or son or daughter. Matthew 19:29 adds, "Every one that hath forsaken houses, or brethren, or sisters, or father, or mother, or wife, or children, or lands, for my name's sake, shall receive an hundredfold, and shall inherit everlasting life."

For the Christian, the relationship with God takes precedence over every other relationship. The requirements of God are to be given first place, even when it means division in the home.

My father and uncle were evangelists on the sawdust trail, during the Chautauqua days, and while I was sitting in the sawdust making airplanes, I would hear them talking about truth. Many times, one person in a family would become convicted to make the decision for Christ, and then they would begin to struggle. A wife would say, "I hear what you're saying, I know it's from the Bible and it's true. But I cannot accept because my husband is not interested. I would rather not be in heaven if my husband is not going to be there."

At first glance, it could sound like a loving decision, couldn't it? How unselfish, to give up eternal life in order to keep peace in the family and stay united with the ones you love.

But I can still remember the answer given, there on the sawdust trail, as my father and uncle dealt with the hard questions. They would paint a picture of the end of time, after the judgment has come, when those who rejected Christ are cast into the lake of fire, prepared for the devil and his angels. And there was the man who refused to accept the truth of God's Word, and with him, his wife—who also refused to accept, because he refused. She loved him too much to go to heaven without him.

As they stand there together, there in the fire, he turns to his wife and says, "You know, Sweetheart, I really appreciate what you've done in coming here with me." And he puts his arms around her and holds her close, because she loved him enough to go to the lake of fire with him.

It's ridiculous, isn't it? Why, he would be cursing the day she turned away from Christ. Perhaps if she had taken a stand, he would have then followed later.

Recently I drove into the driveway of my parents' home, and my father, now in his eighties, met me with this comment, "Son, I've been doing a lot of thinking, and I've decided that I want to be in heaven for Jesus' sake, whether anyone else from my family is there or not."

This was an amazing statement from my father, who has always been a fanatic about his two boys! I can't tell you how many times my brother and I have been embarrassed by some of the things my dad has said in front of us, thinking the sun rose and set on his sons. Now he says, "I want to be in heaven for Jesus' sake, whether my family is there or not." How could he say it? Yet I knew what he was saying. He had been reading these words of Jesus once more and was accepting the invitation to place God first, before anyone else. "He that loveth father or mother, son or daughter, more than me is not worthy of me." Do I love Jesus that much? I want to! I'd like to please my dad and be there too!

In the end, only the one who puts Jesus first, really puts the relatives and family first, setting the example of love and commitment to them.

Jesus wants to get married. Do you? Are you willing to accept His proposal? Or do you write your own? Do you say to Him:

"I am asking You to be my God. However, there are certain qualifications. First, I wish it understood that I love myself more than I do You. My family and friends are also more important to me, which is understandable, I am sure, when you consider that I have known them so much longer than I have You.

"Second, if it comes to a crisis with respect to any basic decision, of course I will consult my own wishes rather than Yours. Some of Your ideas seem very strange to me, and if I am to make a name for myself in the business in which I am employed, I cannot be tied down to Your set of values. I'm sure You understand how I feel.

"Third, I am reserving my right to time of my own. I am a very busy person and cannot be expected to spend time in communion with You day by day. Whatever time I have left over from my business must be primarily spent with my family and friends.

"Fourth, a word about my property. You must realize that it belongs to me exclusively. I find it hard to say goodbye to my money. You own the cattle upon a thousand hills, as well as extensive mining assets, so I can see no reason for You to make any claims on my property or money.

"Oh yes—another thing. I cannot bear sickness, tears, or sorrow. So please do not expect me to enter into fellowship with You in suffering. I have no desire to become involved in service to others. Bear Your own cross, and leave me out of it.

"However, I do want You to be my God. As such, You will have the full responsibility for providing me with salvation, for showering me with blessings, and for answering my prayers. This will free me to give full attention to myself, my family and friends, my possessions, and my business.

"Under the above conditions, I could enjoy having You as my God, and I feel sure we could have some nice times together—maybe on Sabbaths, if I'm not too tired. Will You say Yes? If You do, please begin construction at once on my heavenly mansion. And go ahead with preparation for the marriage supper of the Lamb. I'll plan to be there if I'm not too busy."

Chapter 5
Bless the Children

My father was a disciplinarian of the old school. Where he came from in Norway, they didn't spare the rod. When I was small, he used something light, like a newspaper or a little switch. One day after I had been disciplined, I came back to my mother in the kitchen and said with a little grin, "That didn't even hurt!" That was the worst mistake I ever made!

She relayed the information to my father, and the next time, he made sure to correct for his error! I would tell you that the next time he used the hose off the tire pump—but there have been times when I have admitted that publicly and afterward have gotten letters or phone calls accusing my father of child abuse! But although the instrument he chose to discipline me was enough to make it hurt, it was not enough to cause injury. And there was one thing I always knew, regardless of the discipline I received. I always knew that my father loved me. His love was way ahead of the punishment he gave.

The subject of children, and how to relate to them, is one of the eight big ones that can cause the breakdown of communication in marriage. If two people marry and discover afterward that one of them loves children and wants to fill the house with them, while the other has a motto to hang on the wall that says, "Anyone who hates dogs and kids can't be all bad," then there are going to be problems! They haven't done their homework.

Then there's the question of when to begin the family. Should it be started right away, or should they wait awhile?

41

There have been young people on the verge of separation over that one.

And of course there's the decision of how many children to have—and whether to have boys or girls!

But the biggest question that seems to surface concerning children is the issue of how to bring them up, once they get here. Most often disagreements come in the area of discipline. She grew up on the M&M's and he grew up on the rod. Her parents read Dr. Spock; his parents read Dr. Dobson. And now they have to decide which method to use with their own children.

There is good counsel in Colossians 3:20, 21. "Children, obey your parents in all things: for this is well pleasing unto the Lord. Fathers, provoke not your children to anger, lest they be discouraged." The responsibility for obedience is not only the children's responsibility. It is the father's as well. Obedience without discouragement is the goal. It doesn't seem fair, really, that we don't have one set of children to practice on before the real ones arrive! It is possible for fathers to provoke their children to anger, and then punish them for the anger that they themselves have caused. That's discouraging! How can fathers and mothers know when they have given the wrong discipline or too much discipline? How can they avoid bringing discouragement to their children?

One counselor said, "Most mistakes that children make should never even be noticed—let alone dealt with." If you were to notice them, you might be expected to deal with them. So don't even notice! If a growing child has to become so preoccupied with his failures and mistakes that they become the focus of his attention, he's going to develop emotional problems.

One classic description of how to relate to discipline was given by a family expert when asked, "How much discipline can a child take?"

The response was, "There is no limit to the discipline that anyone can take, as long as the person still knows that he's loved and accepted."

Which means that if all I do is look cross-eyed across the

room at my child and he feels rejected, I've gone too far. But even if I were to follow my father's example in discipline from the old country, so long as my child still knows he's loved and accepted, it will be all right.

I never questioned that I was loved and accepted. How did I know? My father spent quality time with us. Saturday night was called "open night." It didn't matter who was in town. The president of the United States? Forget him! Forget the committees and board meetings and appointments. When Saturday night came, my father was down on the floor, romping with us, playing "roly poly" and "gymnasium" and having fun.

We'd go to bed, and he'd come in and rub our backs. To this day I'm a goner for a back rub. When I go home to visit my parents, the first thing I do is lie down on the living-room floor, while my father rubs my back again.

My father would go to the piano and play some chords, just chords, and sing a song to us:

> Sweetest little fellow, anybody knows.
>   Don't know what to call him,
>   but he's mighty like a rose.
> Looking at his pappy, with eyes so shiny blue.
>   Makes you think that heaven is coming down to you.

You cannot go through childhood with that kind of love and not know that you are accepted. And in that atmosphere of love and acceptance, whatever discipline is necessary has its proper place.

One college did a study of the success, or lack of success, in families. It tried to find out the methods of discipline that had been used in hundreds of families. It found that there were three approaches to discipline. First, discipline with love. Second, discipline without love. And, finally, permissiveness.

The conclusions were remarkable. Of course you would expect that discipline with love was at the top of the list, in terms of successful results. But the second on the list was permissiveness. And discipline without love was the bottom of the list. The conclusion was that if you cannot manage discipline with love, you are better off not trying to discipline at all.

Within the framework of love and acceptance, discipline is necessary and essential in order to train children "in the way they should go." But the first problem of raising the right kind of children is being the right kind of parent. Giving birth to a baby does not make you a parent any more than sleeping in the garage makes you a car! It is possible for parents to try to play the role, but sooner or later that will be insufficient. What is it that makes a true father, a true mother? It is unselfish love. And may I remind you that true love is a fruit of the Spirit— never a fruit of the person. There is no one who can work it up or self-generate it. It is only by the grace of God that anyone, including parents, can be anything but self-centered. If mothers or fathers are going to know this unselfish love, then God is going to have to be the center of their lives.

We are all born with the handicap of being separated from God. We are all born sinful. Even parents who have experienced the new birth and who have known something of the unselfish love of Christ in their own hearts have to deal with children who are born self-centered, just as they were.

Self-centered people don't like to be disciplined. But self-centered people need to be disciplined in order to keep from having chaos and anarchy in the world, or in the home. Obedience and discipline are important for the happiness of society.

To begin with, it might be necessary to discipline by force. The goal is for discipline by force to soon be replaced by the discipline of love. There is no greater discipline in the world than the discipline of love, and it makes force look like nothing by comparison.

Let's look now at the different ages of children and some specific suggestions for discipline at each of the stages of growth.

Those who have done the categorizations have called the ages of one to twelve the "Jesus loves me, this I know" age. It's a beautiful age, with beautiful people. Their simple childish dependence has been used by Jesus as an example of the trust all of us should have in Him.

From thirteen to sixteen we have the "Who am I?" age. The time of self-discovery. The time of wanting to be their own persons.

One time I was invited to a retreat in the Rocky Mountains with a group of early-teens. I asked them to give me a label for their age. They said, "No man's land." If I had called them that, they might have thrown me off the mountain. But since they said it about themselves, it was OK. No man's land. Too old to play and too young to work. Neither child nor adult. Wondering where they would go from here. It's a difficult age.

A further breakdown that has been meaningful for some is to begin with ages one to three, the "attitude age." During the first three years of a child's life his attitudes are largely developed. The attitudes formed during the first three years will influence the rest of the life.

Then they tell us that ages four to twelve make up the "memory age." That's the time when the computer is being programmed, the data is being entered. The attitudes formed have a great influence on how the data is received. That's one reason why Christian education can be so important, in order for the information that is put into the memory of the child to come from a Christian perspective.

Ages thirteen to sixteen is the "decision age," when young people begin to make their own decisions about what they are going to do with their life and what is to be their relationship with God. The decisions are made on the basis of the information already received and the attitudes already formed in the earlier years.

Finally, from ages seventeen to twenty-one and beyond, is the "preparation" age. It is the time when the specific preparation is made to follow through on the decisions and choices which were based on the data and information received and the attitudes originally formed toward life.

Parents often panic during the decision and preparation ages. It may be that they have neglected their work as parents, and they are beginning to reap the results of that neglect. Yet God Himself, whom I understand as a rather wise and knowledgeable parent, lost one third of His children. He took a fearful risk in giving us the power of choice, and it is a solemn fact that when children are given the power of choice, you will win some and lose some. Even if you could be the perfect parent, it is no guarantee that you would win the battle of life with your children. But how often we look desperately toward heaven for help to try and do it right and give our children every advantage possible in making the choices that they have been given to make.

Some principles of discipline that I have gleaned from my own research—and my own mistakes—perhaps would be meaningful to consider. Although listing the rules doesn't take long, it is following them that is hard. For tired parents to apply the right principles day after day requires all of the grace of God they can receive.

1. As we have already noticed, discipline is no good unless it is presented in an atmosphere of love and acceptance.
2. Those involved in discipline must agree. Parents need to have spent quiet moments discussing methods, so that they are agreed on what discipline they are going to use. If they don't, it will be nothing but confusion.
3. Rules should be few, rules should be clear, rules should be reasonable, and rules should be enforceable. Otherwise they are useless.
4. Consistency. One family counselor said, "There are three rules for disciplining children. Consistency, consistency, and consistency." This is a big one. If the rules of the household are enforced today, but not tomorrow, children will become edgy and confused. If the rules are enforced for Susie, but not for Johnny, there will be problems.

If I have to say, "I mean it," I've already lost the battle. If I have to say, "I *really* mean it this time," I have lost bad! The parent who shouts up the stairs, "This is the last time I'm going to say 'this is the last time,' " is advertising that he or she has failed.

A college president said to me one time, "A child's security is in proportion to the predictability of his parents." For the child who knows what to expect, discipline is meaningful.

5. Discipline should be prompt. If a child has to wait until

Dad gets home, the whole issue might have become clouded or forgotten. However, it is a mistake to discipline in anger. If a parent has lost control over his own spirit, it may be necessary to go apart for a little while to gain a fresh hold upon God, in order to discipline calmly and avoid provoking children to the anger that is in the parent's own heart.

6. Teach children the true meaning of self-discipline. If children's only discipline comes when a parent is standing over them, forcing them to submit, they will be like ships without an anchor when those restraints are removed. Self-discipline should be taught as early as possible.

But this leads us to a problem. Some people are strong-willed, and some are not. Some have backbones like gristle, and others have backbones like wet spaghetti. Some may be unable to force themselves to obey. And this is where we need to understand that the better term for self-discipline would be God-discipline. Even the weakest child can learn to surrender himself to God and His control. Control by God is the only kind of true self-discipline that any one of us can experience.

7. Corporal punishment is to be a last resort. Now some of us grew up on the last resort, as we have already mentioned! However, corporal punishment is biblical. "He that spareth his rod hateth his son: but he that loveth him chasteneth him betimes." Proverbs 13:24. Betimes! I don't know how many times that is, but I had all of them! "Chasten thy son while there is hope, and let not thy soul spare for his crying." Proverbs 29:18. Sorry Dr. Spock! "Foolishness is bound in the heart of a child; but the rod of correction shall drive it far from him." Proverbs 22:15. "Withhold not correction from the child: for if thou beatest him with the rod, he shall not die." Proverbs 23:13.

With all the talk today of child abuse, the Bible's talk about the rod seems almost out of place. It's true that there is a lot of child abuse today. The statistics indicate that probably one out of two children experience either abuse or molestation at some point in their childhood. Those are the facts on the subject. It's a sad world in which we live. Any talk about the rod, and not sparing the rod, should not be misunderstood. Children can be abused by parents who never use the rod— but who neglect them, ignore them, or reject them.

So when you are deciding on the form of punishment, remember that corporal punishment should always be a last resort. It is designed to bring discomfort—but it should never bring injury. Any punishment that results in a child needing medical attention has obviously gone too far—no matter what the reason. If you have reached the last resort, and the spanking still has not accomplished its purpose, it is time to seek outside help.

There is one more rule for the discipline of teenagers that we should add before we go on. It is, Roll with the ship. Don't get shook! That's the one rule I've been given over and over again, by parents who have learned from their success, and parents who have learned from their failure. Don't get shook. When your teenager comes in and says he's going to do something crazy, don't overreact. If you do, he'll go ahead for sure. But if you roll with the ship, he'll likely forget about it—and think of something else dumb by tomorrow!

In his senior year of high school, the son of radio pastor H. M. S. Richards would get together with his friends in one half of the garage for jam sessions with their jazz band, while Richards was in the other half of the garage, which was his study—praying!

One day that year, Harold Junior came to his father and said, "Dad, I have finally decided what I want to do when I graduate."

"Really?"

"Yes, I want to have my own jazz band."

"You're sure that's what you want to do?"

"Yes."

"OK, son, as long as you're sure that's really what you want."

And he walked away. No rod. No M&M's. No lectures. Nothing. He just went to his study, and Harold knew what his father was doing in there.

Harold told me that fall, when we became schoolmates at college, that his father's words hit him like a bolt of lightning. "You're sure that's what you want?" "You're sure that's really what you want?" By that fall, he was in college studying to be a minister.

If his father had said, "Over my dead body will you have a jazz band," probably Harold would have one of the best today! Instead, today he has succeeded his father in the radio ministry.

There is power in prayer. And whatever mistakes you make in trying to raise your children, there is one mistake you can never afford to make—and that is to neglect to pray for them. Whatever other areas you miss, don't miss it here. There is power available through prayer that will give you grace and wisdom to do and say the right thing for each situation.

Often parents have asked, "How do we teach righteousness by faith to our children?" It's an important question. We adults find it impossible to live the Christian life if we are unconverted—how can we expect that our children will be able to accomplish it?

There is no easy answer, but here are a few suggestions. First, by example. Christianity is not transferred by heredity. The first thing you can do to assure that your children will give God top priority in their lives is to give God first place in your own life. Your children will know whether or not your private time of communion with God is important to you, or merely an option.

Second, train them from their earliest years to obey you because they love you. Teach them to confess their sins and mistakes to Jesus and seek His forgiveness and power. They can have a relationship with God for themselves that is in keeping with their years—even a tiny child can learn to pray. You can read to them the stories of Jesus long before they are old enough to read for themselves. You can talk more about the love of God than about correct behavior. You can let them know that Jesus loves us when we're good, when we do the things we should, but that Jesus also loves us when we're bad. You can encourage them as early as possible to seek to know Jesus for themselves, not just through your experience.

And through all of their lives, pray for them. Ask the Lord to work in your heart so that nothing you do will hinder your children coming to Him. Ask Him to work in their hearts to draw them to Himself. Seek His wisdom in every situation. He is just as willing to bless the children today as He was when He was here personally.

♥ ♥ ♥

Let's go now to the spiritual side, for we are all His children. Jesus said, "Except ye become converted, and become as little children, ye shall not enter into the kingdom of heaven." Matthew 18:3.

What does that mean? Are we to become childish? No, we don't need that. It means we are to become childlike. It sounds strange to the high achiever, but as we grow into God's kingdom, we don't grow up to stand on our own two feet. The more we grow and the more we mature, the tighter we cling to the hand of our heavenly Father. We grow to dependence, not independence.

It's an inverse pattern. In our families, we expect our children to become more and more separate, independent, their own persons. The ultimate goal is for them to leave our control completely. But not so with God. Adam and Eve tried it on their own, and as a result we're still here. The Creator-creature relationship is still a dependent relationship. It is when we are weak that we are strong. When we think we are strong, we are weak and fall flat on our faces. *Dependence* and *submission* are the key words for Christian maturity.

We experience discipline as children of the heavenly Father. Read it in Hebrews 12. "My son, despise not thou the chastening of the Lord, nor faint when thou art rebuked of him: for whom the Lord loveth he chasteneth, and scourgeth every son whom he receiveth. If ye endure chastening, God dealeth with you as with sons; for what son is he whom the father chasteneth not?" Verses 5-7. And verse 11, "No chastening for the present seemeth to be joyous, but grievous: never-

theless afterward it yieldeth the peaceable fruit of righteousness unto them which are exercised thereby."

Who enjoys chastening? But who can survive without it? It
is in love that the Lord brings His discipline into our lives. Yet
there have been people who have misunderstood and who
have pulled away from relationship with Him because of the
chastening rod.

Christians have debated long over God's role in our discipline. Is He the active agent, or merely a passive parent,
standing aside and allowing the devil to do His work? Some
try to argue for a mild-mannered God who never punishes
anyone. The Old Testament presents a God who is a strong
disciplinarian. Where does God's active role begin and end?

The Bible answer is that justice and mercy are inseparable.
If we ever question God's justice, we need only to go to Cal-
vary and see the offer of mercy that was extended on that day,
to know that God's love and acceptance exceed His justice for
every sinner.

Happy is the one who has learned to know the love of God
and who continues to love and trust Him, in spite of the discipline of life in a world gone wrong.

In one parish a little old lady of eighty was run over by a
truck. Now that didn't particularly make her day. The truck
ran over her upper legs and thighs. She was in the hospital in
great pain, with her legs split open. I went to the hospital to
visit her and try to cheer her up. I didn't want to go. I didn't
know what to say that would help.

But as I walked through the hospital corridor, nearing her
room, I heard someone singing and praising God. It was this
little lady from my church. I couldn't believe it. I thought
maybe it was the morphine or whatever they had given her for
the pain. But she was in her right mind, praising God.

All I could do was stand and stare at her. Finally I found
the words to ask, "Grandmother, I don't understand how you
can be doing this."

She looked at me and said, "Why curse God and die, when
you can praise God and live?"

I went to cheer her up, but ended up being the one who was

cheered by her faith and courage.

Finally, on the divine side of the relationship as it is affected by children let's notice Matthew 19:29. "Every one that hath forsaken houses, or brethren, or sisters, or father, or mother, or wife, or children, or lands, for my name's sake, shall receive an hundredfold, and shall inherit everlasting life." In other words, God says, "Don't let the children come between you and Me."

Parents of young children particularly find it is often easy to allow the demands of the children to interfere with their spiritual life.

We know that any wise parent, with any manners at all, will take a child out of the church service, rather than let the child disturb the rest of the congregation all through the service. Sometimes it seems easier just to stay at home and forget about trying to go to church, when it so often ends up with one or the other parent out in the hallways with the crying child.

Children make unlimited demands upon the time of their parents, and there are young mothers, in particular, who seem to have no time for private devotions, no time for quiet moments to seek God, because the children are always there, always needing something.

Sometimes parents say, "I guess I'll just have to wait five years, or ten, until the children are older, before resuming my own relationship with God." Yet it is during the child's early years that parents are perhaps most in need of the grace of God to aid them in the management of their little ones.

Consider it carefully. The last I heard, even parents of small children find time to eat. They find time to spend alone together. They find time to continue to care for what they consider to be important. Fathers still keep on with their jobs. Many mothers work outside the home as well. Parents still find time to get dressed, to shower or shave, to comb their hair and brush their teeth. Why? Because they consider these things important!

If you really consider your time with God to be top priority, you will find a place for it in your schedule, even when your children are infants.

When our children were small, I determined not to take unfair advantage of my wife and the daytime demands on her time. So I asked the Lord to awaken me in the middle of the night, and in the process discovered that some of the most beautiful times of the day are in the middle of the night! But my wife had the same opportunity at those quiet hours that I did. Some parents have agreed to take turns, as one cares for the needs of the children while the other has some quiet time apart, and then they trade. Whatever method, it should be structured so that both husband and wife have equal opportunity. And God is willing to meet you more than halfway in your attempts to reach that goal. The relationship with Christ one-to-one is equally important for every member of the family. No one can eat for another. Each individual must find the time to seek God for himself.

Children can make it more difficult to seek communion with God, but they can also be a tremendous help in that search. Enoch discovered, after the birth of his own son, that he understood far more of the love of God for His children than he had before, and he was drawn into even closer fellowship with his heavenly Father. In fact, one person went so far as to say that he didn't see how anyone could gain eternal life without having had children. He had been made so much more aware of his own need of God because of having been a parent.

If we continue to seek God and give Him first place in our lives, the experience of having children should draw us closer to God, not separate us from Him. Then we can be used by God to introduce our children to Him, that they may find Him for themselves.

Chapter 6
Chocolate-covered Brussels Sprouts

One couple told me that the only thing they had in common was that they were married by the same minister, in the same church, on the same day. Another couple said that the only thing they had in common was that neither one of them liked chocolate-covered Brussels sprouts—and that's not a whole lot in common!

The lack of common interests between marriage partners can look innocent at first glance. Perhaps you've even heard that opposites attract. Yet every one of the areas where communication can break down is affected by whether or not there are common interests, common backgrounds, common ways.

For instance, how many of the disagreements about money stem from different habits and ideas of how money should be handled? If his mother worked outside the home, but her mother was always there with the cookies and band-aids when the children came home from school, whose example will be followed in the new home?

Even in the simple things of lifestyle, where decisions must be made about how often to eat out, what kind of music to listen to, how much television to watch, differences in background and ideas can cause disagreements between husband and wife. How much more are there disagreements when it comes to the major areas of concern.

The rule applies on every level. The more ideas and ways in common, the greater will be the harmony. The fewer things that are held in common, the greater the potential for breakdown of communication in the marriage.

When a couple comes to me for marriage counseling, one of the first things I do is to go down through the list of the eight major areas where communication most often breaks down, and we discuss whether or not they are having difficulties in each of the areas.

If there seems to be agreement in most areas, but the couple is having a problem in communication on one or two, then usually there is hope of an early solution. But if they can't agree on how to handle the money, if they fight about religion, can't stand the in-laws, argue about how to discipline the children, and so on, I know we're in for a long, hard winter!

To use the same principle, if a couple is considering marriage and there are many areas of common interests and common backgrounds, they can probably work around those things that they do not hold in common. But when there are very few common interests, the chances for disagreements and discord are greater, and they may soon find it easy to go their separate ways.

This is probably the greatest problem when it comes to marriages between those of differing races or cultures. There are so many built-in differences in background and attitudes, that it is often difficult to maintain enough common interests to make the marriage work.

Yet the area of common interests can be deceptive. It often happens something like this: He loves football. She has never cared for football. In fact, she has always hated football. But now she loves him. And what do you know? She has found a new interest: football!

A year later, after the thrill of the romance has cooled, they both discover the real truth of the matter. She still hates football. She always will hate football. Now the lack of common interests makes its mark. While he's watching the football games, she finds something else to do that is more in line with her interests.

Many couples have discovered, to their dismay, that after the flame of infatuation has died down they have very little in common. During the time of courtship, sitting together holding hands may be sufficiently stimulating in and of itself! It may make little difference whether you sit and hold hands at a football game, in church, at a concert, or in the park. But what about the years to come, when marriage has matured the love, and sitting together holding hands is not the novelty it once was? Then what will your interests be?

While it may be relatively easy to adjust to the disappointment of discovering that your mate doesn't share your taste when it comes to something like football, the same pattern can be much more crucial in other areas. For instance, what about when it happens in the realm of spiritual interest and Christian commitment? Perhaps he has never been that interested in spiritual things. But now he loves her—and suddenly, he experiences what looks like conversion! Now he loves God too. But before long they discover to their chagrin that the conversion was only to her—not to her God. And the pull in opposite directions begins in earnest.

I can still remember the couple that came to my office one time who had experienced this very thing. He had never been as interested in spiritual things as she had been. But now he apparently had been converted and loved God. She was certain that his conversion was genuine. It appeared to be. He fooled me too. He may have fooled himself. I remember talking to him about it and quizzing him.

Then I married them. Within three months, it was all over. It didn't take long after the marriage for them to realize that he couldn't have cared less about God or Jesus, and had no faith in spiritual things. He couldn't get out of the marriage fast enough.

I've had just enough of those kinds of weddings in the past that you have to run and catch me in order to get me to perform a wedding anymore! Certainly more than human wisdom is required in order to know which marriages are "made in heaven."

What can be done to avoid this kind of sad awakening? You wait and you wait and you wait. You go on the basis of what the interests have been in the past, *before* you met each other. If there has been a genuine conversion or change in the life that came simultaneously with the present relationship, then you can afford to wait and find out. You cannot afford *not* to! And you stay out of the car, and you stay away from the moon, while you're finding out!

What can be done after marriage and the lack of common ways has taken its toll? Is there a solution even there?

Shortly after I began preaching a series on marriage and family in our home church, my wife confronted me and said, "You've done a good job describing the problem. Now how about telling us something about a solution? What is the answer to the breakdown of communication in marriage?"

It sounds almost too simple to credit—but the solution to the breakdown of communication in marriage is to communicate! The safeguard against future breakdown in communication is to communicate. If you are having problems in communication in any area, you talk about it. You set aside deliberate time to hear and to be heard. The answer to the breakdown of communication in marriage is to communicate.

If you are contemplating marriage, you need to spend time talking about your backgrounds, your tastes, your likes and dislikes. You need to share the details of what your lifestyle was before you met.

In recent times the computer has been used as a shortcut to try to match people according to their interests and personalities. But perhaps on the practical level, the computer falls short. It is not always easy to fall in love with the "right" person.

When I was leaving for college, my parents advised me to marry someone who could play the piano. They felt that it was important for a minister's wife to be able to play the piano— sort of built-in evangelistic equipment! So I went off to school and began to try and fall in love with the pianists on campus. But it didn't work.

Now please, I'm sure there are many lovely pianists in the world. But at that time, in that place, nothing clicked. It took me a while to realize that we wouldn't be spending the rest of our married life on the piano bench! Then one day I found myself attracted to someone who had enough other qualities to make up for her lack of ability at the piano!

Some have felt that the answer to discovering someone with enough interests in common with yours to make a happy marriage is to go to the psychologists and take all of the personality and compatibility tests. But here again, this is not always practical in real life. After all, if a relationship is still in the stages of casual acquaintance, why would you rush out to take the compatibility tests? That could kill it right there! On the other hand, once you have fallen in love and are considering marriage, how easy is it going to be to follow the advice of the test results if they show a lack of things in common? In the beginning the testing is too soon, and in the end it's too late.

Now the counseling center and testing have their place. Even after marriage, the results of this type of testing can open the way for further communication and understanding, not only with your mate, but even with yourself. But it is certainly not a complete answer in itself.

After we had been married for a few years, my wife and I went off to study at the seminary. During that time we became acquainted with a psychologist who had known my parents when they were in school together. He took an interest in my wife and me and volunteered to give us a battery of tests, all for free.

So we sat down and took all of his tests. We took the Minnesota Multiphasic, the Taylor/Johnson Temperament test, the inkblot test, and so on. Many of the things the tests showed about our personalities and interests we already knew. But those things we had not yet discovered were beneficial to learn.

One breakthrough that came my way as a result of what these tests showed was that I realized I had been trying to be something I wasn't, in terms of my role in the ministry. God used this method to guide me in future decisions concerning my goals in His work. Although I had been somewhat skeptical concerning the value of psychological testing prior to that time, I came to understand the importance of knowing more about what makes us tick.

People considering spending the rest of their lives together can receive great benefit from studying the patterns that show up on some of these tests, and they can put that in the portfolio as they try to determine God's will for their future. For those who are already married, it can encourage communication and understanding.

Once a couple realizes a lack of common interests, at least they can agree not to major in the things they don't have in common. They can be more accepting of their partner's differences in interests and opinions, and they can set aside certain times when they are each free to pursue their own interests. Then they can study how to spend as much time as possible on the things they do hold in common.

But it is just logical to conclude that people who end up married to those with whom they have many things in common are going to spend the most time together. And the people who end up married, but having the least common interests, are going to spend the least time together. That's the way it's going to be.

The Bible talks about the need for common interests. "If a house be divided against itself, that house cannot stand." Mark 3:25. Abraham Lincoln applied that text to the American Civil War. But whether you are talking about nations or families or principalities and powers, the same principle still applies. Any house divided against itself cannot stand. When the division in terms of common interests is broad, the house is not likely to stand for very long.

But surely God is better than any computer or test or human wisdom in trying to decide who your future mate should be. If you commit your search to Him, He would be more than able to match you up, not only to one with whom you could have enough things in common on which to build a lasting relationship, but also to one you could truly love.

We were having a discussion about this on one college campus, when a math professor stood up and made a startling suggestion. He said, "The best thing most people could do, in order to find the right mate, is to stop looking—and seek God's guidance, inviting Him to call the shots."

At first it sounded like an almost foolish suggestion. But

then we decided it was probably not nearly so foolish as some of the matchmaking schemes some of us had been involved in. God's track record is pretty good, if you check the Bible account, for being able to bring people together who can find lasting joy and companionship. It's pretty hard to top the story of Isaac and Rebekah—or Ruth and Boaz. Those who have trusted to God's guidance in their choice of a marriage partner have discovered that He knows how to choose for them—to their bliss.

He also stands ready to give extra wisdom and grace for those who are already married, who are seeking to discover how to make the most of their lives together.

Marriage involves work! Have those of you who are married discovered that yet? Communication involves work. And if people would work as hard at finding ways to communicate after they are married as they did before they were married, we would have a lot more happy marriages.

Marriage is based on relationship, and relationship is based on communication, as we have already noticed. Someone wrote the following paragraphs warning about the dangers of taking the relationship for granted.

"Married couples start out on a hopeful level, but soon the young woman begins feeling, Oh well, I have my man. I can relax. I can neglect my hair, my clothes, my house. She turns into a frump"—whatever *that* is! —"and the husband wonders why he indeed married this creature. Ten years later, the husband is gone. The wife is left with the supreme wish that she had acted differently, but it is too late now.

"The husband's responsibility is as crucial as that of the wife, for the wife may come to see her dashing lover as a blob of flesh, a pile of lazy bones lying on a couch looking at a western when he should be planning for the family's future. She may be repulsed by the constancy of the picture, and one day the wife is gone. She can take it no longer. Again, it is too late to recapture the wedding vows.

"Some of us became Christians twenty years ago, but we've done nothing about it since. The romance of expecting Christ's return as though it would be tomorrow has died out, and our religious lives are a monotony of sick routine. We have neglected Christian service, worship, prayer and Bible study, the fellowship with the living God. Our lamps have no oil, and with some it may be too late to find the way. Their smoking wicks smell to high heaven with hostility, gossip, hatred, envy, jealousy, rebellion, unloveliness. They find no enjoyment of God, no fun in His work. Their hope disintegrates to dead works, creeds, ideas, institutions, all of which must never be touched or changed. Their lamps are filled with soot, having no flame. They are burned-out cinders."

♥   ♥   ♥

It is possible, on the divine side, to discover that the "first love" has died, and we have nothing in common with God. Before the sinner comes to Christ in the first place and experiences the miracle of the new birth, there's no way that he's going to have anything in common with God. Romans 8:7 says, "The carnal mind"—or heart—"is enmity against God: for it is not subject to the law of God, neither indeed can be."

God and the sinner have nothing in common. If God were to allow the sinner to enter heaven, it would become a place of misery. It is an evidence of the love of God that the sinner is excluded from heaven, for an eternity spent in the presence of God would be agony for all concerned.

A friend of mine preached a sermon one day entitled "The Man Who Got to Heaven by Mistake." Several people came late for the service and missed his introduction. They went away and began spreading the news that my friend was preaching heresy! They thought he was actually trying to say that people were going to be in heaven by mistake!

But my friend had a good point. Heaven would be torture for the one who had no interests in common with those there, and he would be looking for the first chance, if the gates were left open, to make his escape.

I have sometimes asked audiences a catch question. "How many of you are going to be happy when you get to heaven?" Usually every hand goes up. Then I say, "Not so fast! I didn't ask how many of you would be happy just to have 'made it'—

but how many are going to be happy while you are there?"

A similar gimmick is to suppose there were a button you could press so that you would never sin again. Would you press the button? There are two distinct types of response to this question. The first is, "Quick! Take me to the button!" The other is, "No way! It might ruin my fun."

Sit down sometime and take an inventory of the most important things in your life. Make a list of the five or ten major items that come to mind. Consider how many of those will be available in heaven.

Then make a list of the things that you understand to be important in heaven and decide how many of those you would find enjoyable as well. Our tastes and inclinations will not be miraculously changed when Jesus comes again. If we find that we have little in common with God today, chances are we would not find heaven a comfortable place in which to spend eternity.

What is the center and focus of heaven? Try listing a few of heaven's priorities.

We understand the angels love to spend time in worship and fellowship with God. Is that one of your primary interests?

All heaven works for the good of others. That's what makes heaven, heaven. Even if you have only a surface understanding of the gospel, you know that the salvation of the lost, this one world gone wrong, this one speck in the universe, is a project in which all heaven is absorbed.

There will be a lot of people in heaven out of a job! Physicians will find themselves unemployed. Dentists will have no more business. Undertakers will have to find a new line of work. But there is one profession, one occupation, one vocation that will last forever. It is being involved in service and reaching out to others, sharing the good news of salvation.

Oh, you may say, When Jesus comes again, there'll be no more sinners to reach with the gospel, and so we can all become interested in something else—like hang-gliding! I've always wanted to hang-glide, but my wife is mean! She says I have to choose between her and hang-gliding. So I have decided to save my hang-gliding for heaven! And in heaven I am going to hang-glide without the hang-glider!

Perhaps we will all be kids again when we get there. Can't you see the angels smiling as we practice our touch-and-go's on the sea of glass during the first few days?

But one day you see your angel coming and asking, "Would you like to take a trip?"

"Sure, where are we going?"

"There's a little planet on the outer rim of the universe that wants to hear firsthand the story of what it's like to have been rescued from a world of sin."

You say, "Let's go! Just wait until I pack."

"No, there's nothing to pack!"

"Let me say goodbye to my friends."

"Well, you may want to tell them where you're going, but there's no need to say goodbye, because they will all be here when you return. In fact, they'll be here forever."

So you wing your tireless flights to worlds afar until you reach this little planet the angel told you about. Everyone gathers together to hear what you have to say, while your angel sits on the back row and listens as well. For "angels never felt the joy that our salvation brings."

The song describes it:

There is singing up in heaven
  such as we have never known,
Where the angels sing the praises
  of the Lamb upon the throne.
Their sweet harps are ever tuneful
  and their voices always clear.
O that we might be more like them
  while we serve the Master here.

Holy, holy, is what the angels sing,
  And I expect to help them
make the course of heaven ring;
  But when I sing redemption's story,
they will fold their wings,
  For angels never felt the joys

that our salvation brings.

—*Seventh-day Adventist Hymnal,* no. 425.

Let me ask you this, if our number one interest throughout eternity will be the worship and honor of God and sharing the good news of His redeeming love, wouldn't it be a good thing to get started before that time? If we are going to have enough things in common with those in the heavenly country, we will want to become involved now in working with them in service and outreach.

Chapter 7
Sexual Happiness

This will be a short chapter! The sexual side of marriage is discussed more freely today than in the past, and there are more books on the subject available today in the Christian book stores than there used to be in the stacks at the library where people would hide to look up information!

But the Bible makes it clear that marriage is God's idea. He performed the first marriage in Eden. Marriage is used as an illustration of the close relationship that is to exist between God and His people. There are passages in the Bible dealing with the intimate side of marriage that are almost embarrassingly explicit for the conservative—such as Song of Solomon! So long as we are as discreet—and as open on the subject as is the Bible—we need make no apologies.

Paul gives some very direct counsel to husbands and wives in 1 Corinthians 7, as you may know. Hebrews 13:4 sums up the scriptural attitude toward married love, "Marriage is honourable in all, and the bed undefiled."

But there is one major principle when it comes to the sexual side of marriage. It is a universal and timeless principle that many, even within the Christian church, have missed. It is this: sexual happiness in marriage is the result of a happy marriage, not the cause.

The world at large has it backward. You can find many secular counselors who will advise that if you are having problems in your marriage, just go to bed more often, and that will take care of everything. I've never heard of a greater example of righteousness by works in my life!

It should be shouted from the housetops. "Sexual happiness in marriage is the result of a happy marriage, not the cause."

When couples come to me for marriage counseling, and they confess to problems in every area, right down the list, by the time we get to number five or so, I will say, "And you're having problems in your sexual life, too, aren't you?"

And they are surprised. "How did you know?"

I say, "How could I miss?"

The other of the eight major areas where communication breaks down are more in the "cause" department. This one should most often be classified as a "result." If you are angry or estranged because of breakdowns in communication in any one of the other areas, it will overlap into this one, and there will be a breakdown in communication here as well. But the solution is found in looking for the cause, not in trying to patch up the result. Seldom do you find a marriage that is close and compatible on every other front, but experiencing difficulty in intimacy. Almost always it is coupled with some other factor.

You cannot escape the fact that *you must be close in order to get close.* That's where the sexual revolution missed it to begin with. There is no lasting happiness or security in trying to get close to someone with whom you have only a casual contact. God designed us in such a way that the only real satisfaction of the sexual desires comes when there is union of more than just two bodies—when there is union of mind and spirit as well. It takes far more than geographical location in order for two to become one.

And so, with the exception perhaps of the first few months of marriage, when there may be need for technical information, and even some outside counseling in some cases, the major premise for sexual love is that it is ever, always the result—never the cause—of a happy marriage.

Women seem to have an easier time understanding this principle than men—and some of us raunchy men ought to try to understand it better. Intimacy starts in the kitchen or living room. It's not something you can turn on or off as you come and go to the bedroom. You have to be close in order to get close, and if you're not close, it's hard to get close.

In any marriage, there will be times when you have good feelings. There will be other times when the good feelings are absent. It would be too bad to try to base your marriage on feelings. The feelings come and go. The more intense the feelings, the more short-lived. Our nervous systems would short out if we tried to maintain the most intense feelings for very long. And so the marriage that is based on feelings is destined for failure before very long.

Even though there will be times of good feelings in marriage, we never base our relationship on those feelings. We must find something of more lasting quality on which to base our commitment.

♥   ♥   ♥

That is where we find the bridge into the spiritual side of this topic. Campus Crusade has used an illustration for years, with an engine, a coal car, and a caboose. The engine is labeled "Fact," the coal car is labeled "Faith," and the caboose is labeled "Feeling." The train can never be pulled by the caboose. When the engine and coal car are functioning properly, they can move ahead with or without a caboose.

There are people who have tried to base their entire Christian life on their feelings. Whole churches have operated in this way. They have thought that if they could keep the right kind of music and singing and clapping and maybe a little rolling in the aisles and have the right kind of tear-jerking stories, so that people live on the edge of their nervous systems, then they could have a good religious experience. They believe in righteousness by excitement, righteousness by feeling.

In the Christian life, as in a marriage, there will be times when the feelings are present. In John 14, Jesus said that He would love us and manifest Himself to us. The fruits of the Spirit include love, joy, and peace. Those are feelings. There's nothing wrong with having good feelings. But you can't base your relationship with God on feelings.

When you are having good feelings, thank God for the

bonus. But at times, when the feelings are absent it is no indication that the relationship is over. The only safe course is to continue with your commitment and communication with God, regardless of feelings.

One of the most notable examples of someone who did not depend upon His feelings for His spiritual life was the Lord Jesus Himself. We understand that He was a Man of sorrows and acquainted with griefs. Those sound like feelings. He wept over Jerusalem. He wept at the grave of Lazarus. And in the dark hours in Gethsemane and on the cross, He felt forsaken by His Father. It was only feelings—not fact. In fact, His Father was there with Him, for God was in Christ, reconciling the world unto Himself. Jesus predicted that His Father would not leave Him alone. But He felt alone. He cried out, "My God, why have You forsaken Me?" In the mysterious experience of the atonement, Jesus had to go by more than His feelings. If He had gone just by His feelings, He would have given up the struggle. But He didn't give up.

He remembered the evidences of His Father's love that had already been given to Him. He remembered the Voice from heaven that had spoken, declaring Him to be His Son. He remembered the facts that He had already learned about His Father. He relied upon that, ignoring His feelings. And finally, when His great heart broke, in the last fleeting moments of consciousness, the sense of His Father's presence was restored. Just before He died, He, in essence said, "Father, Father! You're still there. Father, into Your hands I commit My spirit."

There will be times in your Christian life when you won't feel like God is there. But He's there. There will be times when you won't feel like Jesus loves you. But He does. There will be times when you feel as if you are alone and forsaken. But He is with you always, even unto the end.

The Christian is often faced, on a day-by-day basis, with the realization that his feelings aren't that great. You may wake up in the morning, not feeling like getting out of bed and spending that thoughtful time in contemplation of the life of Christ. You may not feel like making the effort for communication and communion with God.

The illustration is used of a man lost in a blizzard, trying to make his way to a place of shelter and safety. He was cold, so cold he thought he wouldn't be able to bear it. Then suddenly, he wasn't so cold anymore. He was tired, and just wanted to lie down on the nice, soft snow and go to sleep. But he'd heard about that! So he denied his feelings and plowed on through the snow until he found his way to safety.

You wake up in the morning. You hear the knock at the heart's door. But the pillow is soft, the bed is warm, and the temptation is to just sink back into the comfort and relax. But you've heard about that! Perhaps you've experienced that too many times already. So you deny your feelings. You go to your closet to seek for the fellowship with God that is the secret of the successful Christian life. And your relationship with God continues.

In marriage, in spiritual life, there is no substitute for taking time for communication, whether you feel like it or not. As you persist in making the time for communication, regardless of feelings, you will discover that the feelings will often come as part of the package.

Chapter 8
The Roles We Play

At age six, I was given the responsibility of being in charge of family worship. That was a real privilege. I had campaigned for that office, and I had a purpose. My plan was to call on the people who prayed short prayers! I remember after several days of that, I figured I'd better be wise and let the ones with the longer prayers have a turn once in a while, or they'd get suspicious! But when it came to family worship, I was in charge.

Who's in charge of your home? Who's supposed to be? Does the Bible say anything about it? Is there an ideal? Let's look at Ephesians 5:22, 23. It's a favorite text for some men! "Wives, submit yourselves unto your own husbands." Then we sort of cough and sneeze our way through the next phrase, "As unto the Lord." And then, "For the husband is the head of the wife." Maybe better leave out the line after that, too, "Even as Christ is the head of the church."

But if we are going to understand the context, and not just pick and choose, we'd better read all of it. "Husbands, love your wives, even as Christ also loved the church, and gave himself for it." This is the kind of husband who would be willing to die for his wife. Maybe it would cut down on a lot of criticism, inside of the home, and outside as well, if we wouldn't criticize anyone unless we were first willing to die for them. "So ought men to love their wives as their own bodies. He that loveth his wife loveth himself. For no man ever yet hated his own flesh; but nourisheth and cherisheth it, even as the Lord the church." Verses 25, 28, 29.

The underlying context of this passage comes from verse 18, "Be filled with the Spirit." Only those who are filled with the Spirit will be able to do it right. And if that is true, then we're not just talking about a certain gender, because verse 21 talks about submitting ourselves one to another in the fear of God. Jesus, the humble Traveler from Galilee, knew what it was like to submit Himself, even to His own disciples. This is the Christian principle.

The last verse of the chapter, verse 33, "Nevertheless let every one of you in particular so love his wife as himself; and the wife see that she reverence her husband." The love and respect is intended to go both ways.

Well, people who are not filled with the Spirit have often taken things out of this chapter and tried to justify becoming domineering tyrants, trying to make a doormat out of their mates. We have those who rebel against that kind of control. And the time has come, both within and without the church, that women are campaigning for equal rights. But the Bible makes it clear that there is a principle involved, an ideal.

There's a second passage that deals with this, found in Colossians 3:18. "Wives, submit yourselves unto your own husbands, as it is fit in the Lord."

And one more text, 1 Peter 3:1-7. We can leave the adornment and jewelry out of it for the moment, and read verses 1 and 7. "Ye wives, be in subjection to your own husbands." "Ye husbands, dwell with them according to knowledge, giving honour unto the wife, as unto the weaker vessel, and as being heirs together of the grace of life; that your prayers be not hindered."

Well, what do you conclude when you read these texts, as far as what is the Bible ideal, the Bible principle? There are some who have tried to make a moral case out of it and insist that a woman's role has particular dimensions, and she must not deviate from it. But there are others who realize that the details may vary, as long as there is agreement between husband and wife as to what their roles include. There were many Bible case histories of women who were given special work by the Lord. We could list Deborah, the prophetess, who led the armies of Israel to victory; Lydia, the seller of purple, who was in business for herself; Miriam, who was Moses' assistant in taking Israel from Egypt to the Promised Land; and even Mary the mother of Jesus, whose role in the plan of salvation puts her husband Joseph in the background.

Husbands are invited to honor and love and cherish their wives, and not to stand between them and their relationship and responsibility to God. But the Bible principle seems to be that when there is a need for one or the other to submit, the wives are invited to lead out in that department, so long as it does not conflict with their duty to God.

If men had loved their wives, and loved them as Christ loved the church, there would never have needed to be a women's-rights movement in the first place. How long has it been since you have read the description of love in 1 Corinthians 13? It describes a Christian love to which anyone would delight to submit.

"This love of which I speak is slow to lose patience—it looks for a way of being constructive. It is not possessive. . . . Love has good manners and does not pursue selfish advantage. It is not touchy. It does not keep account of evil or gloat over the wickedness of other people. . . . Love knows no limit to its endurance, no end to its trust, no fading to its hope; it can outlast anything. Love never fails." 1 Corinthians 13:4-7, Phillips.

Would it be hard to submit to that kind of love, that kind of atmosphere? May I propose that it would not be hard to do. This love that Jesus has for His church is the kind of love that brings motivation for us to do things that we otherwise could not do.

Even within the limits of a loving relationship, there are going to be differences in temperaments, differences in backgrounds, differences in personalities. The experts tell us that we are tremendously influenced by the model of the home in which we grew up ourselves. If someone has a dominant father and a submissive mother, he is either going to be looking for the same sort of arrangement in his own home, or, if he disliked the roles he knew at home, he may do a reverse play and do just the opposite. Your reaction to your past environment has a lot to do with whether you will seek a replica or a reverse.

The four types of temperaments are sanguine, choleric, melancholy, and phlegmatic. These are not modern inventions, but borrowed from the Greek philosophers, who had apparently done a lot of study on the subject, even in their day. A simpler division has been made more recently by one writer who says everyone is either a skunk or a turtle. Skunks are the dominant, take-charge types; turtles are the meek and submissive ones.

♥   ♥   ♥

Once again, there is a parallel on the divine side. A misunderstanding of roles in our relationship with God can cause a breakdown of communication that can ultimately destroy the relationship itself.

Do you know what God expects from you? Do you know what you can expect from Him? What does He do, and what are you supposed to do? What is the relationship of divine power and human effort? These are practical questions; too many new Christians have missed the answers. They began the Christian life with an excitement about the free down payment that was made for them at the cross, but soon discovered that the monthly payments were going to finish them off. They never understood the good news that Jesus made provision not only for the down payment, but for the monthly payments as well. They never heard the good news that not only is forgiveness free, but power for living the Christian life is also freely provided.

How does this work out in practical life? How do we get shoes on it? Let's look at the minicourse in salvation by faith, just two texts. "Without me ye can do nothing." John 15:5. It's not talking about getting your name in lights or making a million. It's talking about the issues of sin and righteousness. Without Jesus, we can do nothing toward obtaining salvation or living the Christian life. We might produce an external goodness, but it doesn't count in heaven. We cannot do one thing toward righteousness apart from Christ. Nothing.

Add to that Philippians 4:13. "I can do all things through Christ which strengtheneth me." If these two texts are true, then the only thing we can do, as our part, is to get with Christ. If without Him we can do nothing, but with Him we can do all things, then all we can do is get with Him. That's our role. That's where the deliberate effort comes in the Christian life.

There is something for us to do. The Bible promise is, "Ye shall seek me, and find me, when ye shall search for me with all your heart." Jeremiah 29:13. God never made provision for us to sit in the rocking chair, while He seeks Himself for us. If He had made such a provision, it would take away our power of choice. To seek Him is our department, even though He invites our seeking, standing at the heart's door and knocking for admission.

It is an absolute necessity, as well as a privilege, to take time to communicate with God, just as it is in our other human relationships. Without communication, there is no relationship. That's where the deliberate effort goes: toward setting aside time for prayer and the study of His Word day by day, in order to seek a genuine relationship with Him.

Then there are all kinds of spontaneous efforts that come as a result. The Christian life is not effortless. We do not believe in a do-nothing religion. But the power of God in us will produce spontaneous effort, not the effort that we must try to grit our teeth and force to happen.

What is spontaneous effort? Perhaps an illustration or two would be the easiest way to explain.

I went to visit a rattlesnake farm once. The man who milked the rattlesnakes was bitten. As he let the snake go, the snake got him in the leg. He whipped out his knife and cut his leg to the bone, as quick as a flash. He knew about the danger, and it was easier for him to cut his leg to the bone than not to. It was spontaneous effort, but it was painful effort. I've wondered if I could do it.

Jerome, the friend of John Huss, thought it was too hard to be burned at the stake. He recanted instead. Then he discovered that it was harder *not* to burn at the stake. So he recanted his recantation and went to the stake spontaneously. Being burned at the stake is not easy—but unnumbered martyrs have found it easier to burn than not to.

This is far more than cooperation. It involves far more than our doing part of the work, and Christ's coming in where we fall short. Without Him, we can do nothing. It has never been true that God helps those who help themselves, when it comes to the issues of salvation. In the spiritual life, God helps those who cannot help themselves.

Are you questioning what areas of your life God has promised to handle for you and what things you must do yourself? There is a simple key. What has God promised? He has never promised to take out your garbage or study for your history exam or seek Himself for you. He has promised to fight sin and the devil for you, so long as you depend upon His strength instead of your own. He has promised to give you victory. He has promised eternal life. He has promised to change your heart.

We accept His promised gifts by coming into His presence and seeking the relationship with Him. If you have tried that and it hasn't seemed to work for you, don't bother trying anything else. There is nothing else. Christianity apart from the relationship with Christ is impossible.

If you are having problems in communication in your marriage, you don't quit communicating. You keep on with the communication. You try to find new methods that may work more effectively. You seek every opportunity to open the door for more meaningful communication.

It is the same in the relationship with God. If your devotional life is losing its power, look for new methods. Try to listen to what God might be telling you as to what the problem might be. But don't stop. That is the last thing in the world you should do.

Perhaps there is something else in your life that is running interference with your time alone with God. For many people, it's the television. They find all kinds of time for watching TV, but somehow can't find the time to spend a quiet hour alone with God.

Early in our marriage, we purchased a television set. Of course, we were only going to watch Walter Cronkite, the coronation of Queen Elizabeth, and perhaps a religious broadcast or two. Then we added a program for the kiddies, and a special nature broadcast.

It really wasn't very long before the night I came home from prayer meeting and stayed up to watch the late, late show. It was a murder mystery, but it was OK, because there was a missionary in it!

The next morning, it seemed the Bible wasn't nearly as interesting as it once had been. Have you ever had that happen? It's very real. So I cut the plug off the end of the television cord!

But Queen Elizabeth was crowned again, or something like that, and my wife stripped the wires and put them into the socket. Fire flew, and she thought it was a judgment from God! I didn't want any more of that, so I put the cord and the plug back together. But that wasn't the end of it. The cycle repeated, until when we finally sold the set, it had a six-inch cord!

A friend of mine decided his television was ruining his relationship with God, and he didn't want it doing the same for anyone else. He was a heavy-equipment operator, so he took his backhoe, dug a deep hole, dropped his color television set in the hole, and covered it over with dirt!

Does it take energy to do that sort of thing? Sure it does. Was there effort involved? Yes. But he would have had to try harder not to do it, because of his desire for the greater good. That is spontaneous effort.

We've just touched the surface of the subject of divine power and human effort. If you would like to pioneer in the area of truth, here's one that's almost untouched. There has been all kinds of research and study and books written and sermons preached on the subject of the proper use of the will preconversion, at the beginning of the Christian life. But we have left everyone more or less on his own when it comes to how to live the Christian life. Study it. A correct understanding of the roles of the Christian and God will make all the difference in your relationship with Him.

We were talking about this subject in a college class one day, and one of the students asked, "Why is it so complicated?"

Well, it really isn't so complicated. We are the ones who have made it complicated, and in trying to make it simple again, it can sound complicated! But the gospel is wonderfully simple and simply wonderful.

The bottom line is that since we can do nothing of ourselves, except get with Christ and seek to know Him, then that's where we put our effort and our deliberate choice. We make the fellowship and communion with Him the top priority of our lives. We don't start out the door in the morning and say, "Oh, I forgot to have my devotions!" Our entire day centers around the private time with Him. Nothing else runs interference with it. It takes second place to nothing.

As we continue to seek Him day by day, He will lead us just as fast as He can to the experience of complete dependence and submission to Him, and teach us how to allow Him to control our lives. This promise is still good for today: "He which hath begun a good work in you will perform it until the day of Jesus Christ." Philippians 1:6.

Chapter 9
When You Are in the Right

Still sits the school house by the road
A ragged beggar, sunning
Around it still the sumac grow,
And blackberry vines are running.

Within the master's desk is seen,
Deep-scarred by raps official;
The warping floor, the battered seats,
The jack-knife's carved initial.

The charcoal frescoes on the wall,
The door's worn sill betraying,
The feet that creeping slow to school
Went storming out to playing.

Long years ago, the winter sun
Shone over it at setting,
Lit up the western window panes,
And cold eves' icy fretting.

It touched the tangled golden curls
And brown eyes full of grieving,
Of one who still her steps delayed
When all the school was leaving.

6—L.M.A.R.

For near her stood the little boy
Her childish favor singled,
His cap pulled low upon a face
Where pride and shame were mingled.

Kicking with restless feet the snow
To right and left he lingered,
While nervously her tiny hands
The blue-checked apron fingered.

He saw her lift her eyes, he felt
The soft hand's light caressing.
He heard the murmur of her voice,
As if a fault confessing.

"I'm sorry that I spelt the word,
I hate to go above you.
Because," the brown eyes lower fell,
"Because you see, I love you."

Still memory to a gray-haired man,
That sweet child's face is showing.
Dear girl, the grasses on her grave
Have forty years been growing.

He lived to learn, in life's hard school
How few who go above him,
Regret their triumph, and his loss
Like her, because they loved him.

The girl who inspired this poem by John Greenleaf Whittier
had learned early an important lesson. She knew how to say
she was sorry—and mean it. Do you know how to say you're
sorry? Have you ever been told to say you were sorry, when
you weren't? When was the last time you said you were sorry
and really meant it? What made the difference?

Studying the major ways in which communication breaks
down leads finally to the subject of reconciliation. In a world of

sin, knowing how to say you're sorry—and more important, knowing how to *be* sorry, is vitally important.

When I was a boy my father and uncle held evangelistic meetings in places like Carnegie Hall, in New York City. They got the idea one time that it would be really spectacular to have white suits and white ties and white shoes against a dark-blue-velvet background. They had seen another evangelist who looked that way.

So they went out and bought all of this white. But somehow, when they wore it themselves, they felt stupid. So the white suit ended up in the closet and the white shoes in the back row, and there they stayed for some time.

One day my mother took the white shoes and gave them to charity, and that's the closest thing to a fight I ever remember between my father and mother!

A few years ago our son was engaged to be married and brought his fiancée home for a visit with my folks and the whole family. Shortly after we arrived, my mother leaned forward and asked the engaged couple, "Have you had a good fight yet?"

My father was aghast. He said, "That's no way to talk! We've never had a fight."

I wanted to say, "What about the white shoes?"

But he said to my mother, "Look at how many years we have been married, and we've never had a fight."

My mother said, "Oh yes, we have."

"No, we haven't!"

"Yes, we have!"

And our boy looked at them and said, "Is this your first?"

My mother went on to say that the reason she asked such a question was because the good thing about a fight is the making up afterward and the good feeling that comes.

Would it be a good idea for those who are planning to be married to be sure to have a good fight, so they are not surprised afterward? Do you believe that fights are inevitable? It might be better, before marriage, to have some practice in learning how to deal with them.

What about those people who have been married for 150

years, who claim that they've never had a fight? They have a bigger problem—it's called amnesia! Or possibly baldfaced lying!

Of course, there are different definitions of what it takes to be called a fight. Some people call simple differences of opinion a fight. For others, a fight is a short argument. For still others, it's not really a fight until the frying pan goes through the plate-glass window!

Differences of opinion are inevitable in all human relationships in this world, whether you're talking about marriage and family or roommates in college or neighbors or friends or the church family or institutions. The Bible gives examples of differences of opinions between those who seemed to be equally committed to Christ, such as Paul and Barnabas and their disagreement over John Mark's role in their ministry. So for those who are contemplating marriage, or who are newly married, the question is not *if* there will be conflicts, but *when*.

Some Bible counsel on the subject of disagreements is found in Ephesians 4:26. It is short and to the point. "Be ye angry, and sin not." So apparently it is possible to be angry without sinning. Then comes the phrase on which the old adage has been based: "Let not the sun go down upon your wrath." Don't go to sleep until you've made up. It's easy to agree with the principle, perhaps harder to follow it when you find yourself in the middle of a fight!

From the study that I have done on this subject, not to mention my own personal experience, I would like to suggest a few rules for successful fighting! Perhaps the best beginning for reconciliation is to fight correctly in the first place!

1. Don't talk about your differences when other people are present.

2. Don't talk about your differences when you are tired or when you are hungry. Wives, if you plan to fight with your husband, feed him first! That might cut short a lot of fights! Most of us find it easier to be disagreeable when we are under stress or when we are tired or hungry. But if you follow these first two rules, you would almost have to plan your fights, which might be a novel idea for some! Perhaps if our fights

were planned, rather than simply spontaneous, we would have fewer of them.

3. When you are discussing a problem, don't attack the other person's personality or character. Limit your remarks to the subject at hand, and don't try to win by tearing down the other person as a person.

Probably no one knows better than one's mate the other person's weak points, and the temptation may be to use that knowledge during an argument in order to attack the other person. But the words of the old poem have a lot of truth:

Boys flying kites haul in their white-winged birds,
But you can't do that when you're flying words.
Thoughts unexpressed may sometimes fall back dead,
But God Himself can't kill them, once they're said.

I saw a film one time in which two different scenes were done to show the two kinds of fighting. In one, the husband and wife, a younger couple, were really going after it, hammer and tongs. They were yelling and screaming at each other— but about the problem, about the issues. They ended up in each other's arms.

In the other scene, an older couple didn't even raise their voices. But every sentence was a barb about the other's personality and person. You could feel it going deep. They ended up more estranged than before.

On this planet Earth, particularly within the Christian church, we had better be prepared for differences and learn what we can about acceptable methods for reconciliation, because we're going to need them! The married world at large doesn't have to fight anymore. They just get out. If you believe that marriage is open-ended, then when there are disagreements you just call it quits.

If you believe that marriage is open-ended, it won't be long before you find ample opportunity to check out. But for the Christian who accepts the Bible premise that marriage is for keeps, that is not one of the options.

The Bible recognizes only two legitimate reasons for ending

a marriage, other than the death of the mate. One is found in Matthew 19—unfaithfulness to the marriage vows. The other is in 1 Corinthians 7—for those who are married to unbelievers.

Since the Christian marriage is not open-ended, we had better be ready to face conflict and know how to use it constructively and how to reconcile when reconciliation is needed. In the Christian marriage, when we have problems, we don't change marriage partners, we change dispositions. We learn how to reach reconciliation when there have been differences, and there is grace from above to accomplish that.

Because of the disagreements that arise, reconciliation is essential. One couple came to my office and confessed to a marriage that was about over. They had been married for twenty years, but now they were in great trouble. This was their final attempt to make it work.

We went down through the list and, surprisingly, it went pretty well. Money? No problem. Religion? Compatibility there. In-laws? Children? Everything was peaceful with the relatives. So on, down the list, until this last one—reconciliation. Then we discovered that they had no acceptable method for reconciliation when there were differences. For twenty years, neither one of them had ever known what it was like to say, "I'm sorry, I goofed. Will you forgive me?"

The unresolved differences had eaten away at the very heart of their marriage, until there was no love left, and the marriage was about over.

The experts tell us that one of the most dangerous things to married love is bottled-up resentment. This couple had a full share over the years, and it had taken its toll. It had all but destroyed a marriage which from every other perspective should have been happy and fulfilling.

Sometimes it takes a lot of communication in order to discover and agree upon an acceptable method of reconciliation. Since our backgrounds are not all alike, what works for one couple may not work for another. There is no single answer that will fit every marriage.

My wife and I discovered this truth on our honeymoon! I

made a dumb remark about her knit dress. I didn't like the knit dress and had the poor judgment to share that thought!

I had forgotten that it was her mother who had knit the dress, and she had lived with her mother a good deal longer than she had lived with me at that time. If I didn't like the dress that her mother had knit, I probably didn't like her mother, either—and all of a sudden I realized that I was in big trouble!

As soon as I became aware of my mistake, I said, "I'm sorry." In the home in which I grew up, as soon as we realized that we had hurt someone or made some mistake, the thing to do was to say you were sorry. And then you kept on trucking!

My wife, however, was used to a different method. It's called the silent treatment. When there had been disagreements, it was nothing but "Pass the salt" for three days. At the end of that time, you began speaking again and went on as if nothing had happened.

But three days is a long time when you're on your honeymoon! When you drive along, hour after hour, with her looking out that side of the car, and you looking out this side, things can get pretty heavy. I thought my marriage was all over, right there on our honeymoon! I learned then that the three-day method was not a method that I was going to be able to live with.

For my wife, however, it hadn't helped that much for me to say I was sorry. She knew better. It takes three days to get sorry!

Well, as soon as we began talking again, we took time to talk about this one. She listened to my feelings and to my story of how I could not stand three days of silence—on our honeymoon or any other time. I listened to her story and tried to understand her feelings. And we began to work out our own system for reconciliation.

What are the methods of reconciliation that have been used? One method is to act as though nothing has happened. That method had been used, unsuccessfully, by the couple who came to my office, ready to end their twenty-year marriage. It didn't work.

We might question whether the Christian should avoid conflict. After all, doesn't the Bible say, "If it be possible, as much as lieth in you, live peaceably with all men"? Romans 12:18. Some have gotten the idea that the only "Christian" thing to do is to avoid conflict at all costs, and they are almost afraid to hold an opinion for fear someone will disagree with them. Do you have to be a marshmallow in order to be a Christian?

Well, there is certainly much to be said for not hitting everything in life head-on. Even for those who are the "skunks," surely there can be some differences of opinion that are not worth major confrontation. We would not want to encourage using conflict as the first resort in every situation, and, in fact, if both husband and wife are trying to please the other and are keeping the needs of the other in mind, it will certainly minimize the conflict in the relationship.

But perhaps a better word than *conflict* would be *confrontation*. The Bible does not recommend ignoring facts or hiding your head like an ostrich. In His dealings with people, Jesus was often open and painfully direct. And it is in communication that we find the answer to the breakdown of communication. Through the avenue of communication, many of the problems that would otherwise prove insurmountable can be solved.

So it is not always necessary, or wise, to act as though nothing has happened, although there may be some issues that are simply not worth fighting over.

The second method, recommended in Scripture, is to acknowledge our guilt, our wrong, and ask forgiveness. The Bible recommends being willing to say, "I'm sorry. Please forgive me." A sincere apology can go far toward bringing healing and reconciliation.

A third method is the silent treatment. Have you ever used that method? How did it work for you? It can be an acceptable method for some, if both parties are agreed. You may even find some Bible support for the silent treatment, times when God had tried every way possible to reach people with message after message calling them to repentance. And finally He became silent. See 1 Samuel 28:6 and Matthew 26:62, 63, for a couple of examples you might want to ponder.

A fourth method that people have used is to compromise. Give and take. You give a little, your mate gives a little, and you meet somewhere in the middle. This can get complicated, however, even though it works for some, for there can be conflict over where the middle line is.

One college professor, who taught the marriage and family class, said that to try for a fifty-fifty compromise is never enough. That marriage is more than a fifty-fifty proposition. He said there may be some days when one partner or the other is incapable of going fifty-fifty. Maybe they can only go forty or thirty or ten. And then there will be a breakdown in the relationship. Couples should plan on the rule being a hundred-hundred proposition, so that ideally there will be enough of an overlap to compensate for the times when one or the other is not doing well.

A fifth method for reconciliation is to agree to disagree. For some types of disagreements, particularly in the realm of the abstract—such as politics—this may be a workable method. He's a Republican; she's a Democrat. After about so many times of arguing back and forth, they agree to disagree. Each acknowledges the other's right to his own views, and they agree not to keep endlessly rehashing the issues.

This method is perhaps more successful when the husband and wife are able to be truly tolerant of the other's views, instead of being only accommodating and exerting that kind of pressure. Tolerance you can live with. Accommodation you may not.

Perhaps one of the greatest aids to resolving conflict is to keep your sense of humor! What would happen to us if we didn't know how to laugh—even at ourselves? With all of the complexity and insanity of life on planet Earth, if we couldn't laugh, we would all go jolly round the bend!

Maybe that's what was behind one couple's method of reconciliation—a reconciliation rug. They dedicated a special little throw rug in the entryway of their home and called it the "reconciliation rug."

Whenever there was a problem or a disagreement or an argument, they would run for the reconciliation rug. The first one there had the advantage, but by the time they both managed to get onto the rug, they were both laughing. Since the rug was so small, in order for both of them to be on the rug, they had to be in each other's arms, which was not a bad idea, either! You might want to try it!

Finally, a major method for reconciliation for the Christian is prayer. This means more than simply a quick prayer with the kiddies before bedtime. The husband and wife who know what it means to pray together have a tremendous advantage in their search for harmony in the home.

Charles W. Shedd, known for books like *Letters to Karen,* did a survey some years ago and discovered that the divorce rate among couples who prayed together was overwhelmingly less than that of even Christian couples. After hearing these figures, he began to analyze his own counseling records and made the amazing discovery that out of more than 2,000 cases, over twenty years of counseling, he had never once met a couple with marriage trouble who prayed together. He said that perhaps a dozen said, We used to.

What does this tell us? That there is power to help with the differences in the Christian marriage. Are there going to be disagreements? Yes, there will be. Should we deny them? No, they must be faced in order to be resolved. But to be able to pray together about the difficulties makes a tremendous difference.

Which of the methods that we have listed are best for you? Probably the answer is that most couples will use all of the methods at some time or another, some more than others.

Some of us attended a seminar one time where the counselor asked the question, "When there have been differences, who should initiate reconciliation—the one in the right or the one in the wrong?"

We all said, "The one in the wrong."

He said, "Wrong! The one in the wrong is emotionally incapable of taking the first step. It must always be the one in the right who initiates reconciliation."

The next time my wife and I had a disagreement, we ran into each other initiating reconciliation—we both thought we were in the right! We laughed and said, "He was tricky, wasn't he? He sure played a fast one on us."

But it can be hard work to take the first step at reconciliation, even when you are in the right. I know—I've done it
many times!

♥   ♥   ♥

But this truth brings us to the spiritual application of this
last major area where communication can break down. Long
ago, God and man were estranged. It's not right to say God
was estranged, because He wasn't. But man was.

Who took the first step in reconciliation? The one who was
in the wrong or the One who was in the right? You know the
answer. You can read it in Romans 5:6-8. "When we were yet
without strength, in due time Christ died for the ungodly. For
scarcely for a righteous man will one die: yet peradventure for
a good man some would even dare to die. But God commen-
deth his love toward us, in that, while we were yet sinners,
Christ died for us."

Listen to it again in the beautiful words in Ephesians 2:4-7.
"God, who is rich in mercy, for his great love wherewith he
loved us, even when we were dead in sins, hath quickened us
together with Christ, (by grace ye are saved;) and hath raised
us up together, and made us sit together in heavenly places in
Christ Jesus: that in the ages to come he might shew the ex-
ceeding riches of his grace in his kindness toward us through
Christ Jesus."

This is the heart of the gospel. Christ initiated reconciliation. And it's been good news for sinners ever since.

Now, of all things, we are invited in 2 Corinthians 5 to join
Him in His work of reconciliation. "Now then we are ambas-
sadors for Christ, as though God did beseech you by us: we
pray you in Christ's stead, be ye reconciled to God." Verse 20.

Christ took the first step. We were incapable of doing anything. He took the first step, and love begets love. Now those
of us who have been in the wrong can have our hearts sof-
tened and subdued by the One who loves us in spite of us. Our
merciful Saviour has never held it against us that we were
born in this sinful world. He is not trying to see how many

people He can keep out of heaven, but rather He is trying to see how many He can get in.

As we come to know and understand the love and acceptance that He has for us, we will be free to offer that same loving acceptance to those around us, beginning with those in our own homes.